MW01001320

PROMOTING TEACHER REFLECTION IN SECOND LANGUAGE EDUCATION

Taking the concept and the practice of reflective teaching forward, this book introduces a well-structured, flexible framework for use by teachers at all levels of development, from pre-service to novice to the most experienced. The framework outlines five levels of reflective practice—Philosophy; Principles; Theory-of-Practice; Beyond Practice—and provides specific techniques for teachers to implement each level of reflection in their work. Designed to allow readers to take either a deductive approach, moving from theory-into-practice, or an inductive approach where they start from a practice-into-theory position, the framework can be used by teachers alone, in pairs, or in a group.

Thomas S.C. Farrell is Professor, Department of Applied Linguistics, Brock University, Canada.

ESL & Applied Linguistics Professional Series

Eli Hinkel, Series Editor

Visit www.routledge.com/education for additional information on titles in the ESL & Applied Linguistics Professional Series

PROMOTING TEACHER REFLECTION IN SECOND LANGUAGE EDUCATION

A Framework for TESOL Professionals

Thomas S. C. Farrell

Routledge
Taylor & Francis Group

NEW YORK AND LONDON

First published 2015
by Routledge
711 Third Avenue, New York, NY 10017

and by Routledge
2 Park Square, Milton Park, Abingdon, Oxon OX14 4RN

Routledge is an imprint of the Taylor & Francis Group, an informa business

© 2015 Taylor & Francis

First edition published by Routledge 2015

Library of Congress Cataloging-in-Publication Data
Farrell, Thomas S.C. (Thomas Sylvester Charles)
Promoting Teacher Reflection in Second-Language Education : A Framework for TESOL Professionals / Thomas S.C. Farrell.
   pages cm. — (ESL & Applied Linguistics Professional Series)
   Includes bibliographical references and index.
  1. English teachers—Training of.   2. English language—Study and teaching—Foreign speakers.   3. Test of English as a Foreign Language—Evaluation.
4. English language—Ability testing.   5. Reflective teaching.   6. Career development.   I. Title.
   PE1128.A2F285 2015
   428.0071—dc23
   2014022489

ISBN: 978-1-138-02503-5 (hbk)
ISBN: 978-1-138-02504-2 (pbk)
ISBN: 978-1-315-77540-1 (ebk)

Typeset in Bembo
by Apex CoVantage, LLC

Printed and Bound in the United States of America by
Edwards Brothers Malloy on sustainably sourced paper.

CONTENTS

FIGURES AND TABLES

FIGURES

TABLES

PREFACE

Reflective practice is now used in many different professions such as the legal profession, nursing, and education. For example, reflective practice has been cited as being especially helpful for students of law who lack practical experience because they can, as Anzalone (2010: 86), has noted, "Examine and test beliefs and principles against what is being learned doctrinally." Within the nursing profession reflective practice has been cited as important because it can help "narrow the gap between theory and practice . . . to discover knowledge embedded in practice" (Kim et al., 2010: 159). Within the field of education reflective practice has had a major impact on virtually all areas of a teacher's life from teacher education programs for novice teachers to professional development programs for experienced teachers. Indeed, in the field of education recently Zwozdiak-Myers (2012: 3) pointed out that reflective practice is central to a teacher's development because it helps teachers "to analyse and evaluate what is happening" in their classes so that they can not only improve the quality of their teaching, but also provide better opportunities for their students to learn. Reflective practice has also impacted the field of second language education and especially the field of teaching English to speakers of other languages (TESOL). Since its emergence in TESOL, reflective practice has become a very popular term in many pre-service and in-service programs worldwide. Although most educators still agree that some form of reflection is a desirable practice among teachers, there is still less agreement on the precise definition of reflective practice, how to do it, and as yet no overall framework exists that all teachers can implement. Hence the main reason I have written this book.

Promoting Teacher Reflection in Second-Language Education: A Framework for TESOL Professionals provides such an overall framework that all second language teachers regardless of the level of their teaching experience can use to reflect on practice.

The framework outlines five-stages/levels of reflections that start at level 1: Philosophy; level 2: Principles; level 3: Theory of Practice; level 4: Practice; level 5: Beyond Practice. Readers can begin their reflections using the framework at any stage or level. For example, they can take a deductive approach to reflection and move from a Theory-into-(beyond)practice mode through the different levels, or they can take an inductive approach where they move from a (Beyond) Practice-into-theory mode through the levels. Indeed, they can also just reflect at one level and stay there depending on the level of interest and the amount of time they have to reflect.

This framework has really taken me 35 years to develop, as it contains all of those years of my reflections on reflective practice. I developed the framework from all the years of not only reading and writing about the concept of reflective practice but also working and reflecting with teachers all over the world. I have had the honor of reflecting with many teachers over the years in many different countries and contexts and they have added to my understanding of what reflective practice is. For example, this year alone (2014) I have been so lucky to be invited to speak and give workshops on reflective practice in Dubai, United Arab Emirates, USA, Singapore, Thailand, UK, Australia, and Japan, and meeting and reflecting with all these wonderful professionals has continued to shape my understanding of what it means to reflect. I have attempted to incorporate all of my travel experiences into the framework I present in this book.

Outline of Book

Promoting Teacher Reflection in Second Language Education: A Framework for TESOL Professionals is made up of nine chapters.

Chapter 1, "Getting into Reflective Practice," is an introductory chapter that sets the scene for the remainder of the book. It explains where and how I developed the new *Framework for Reflecting on Practice* developed from my many years of work with the concept of reflective practice. I briefly outline the five stages/levels of the framework, and how it is unique because it can be used by all language teachers regardless of their level of teaching experience.

Chapter 2, "Contemplation and Reflection," outlines and discusses various aspects of contemplation, reflection, and reflective practice. The main purpose of the chapter is to introduce the key concepts in teacher reflection (inside and outside TESOL), both from a theoretical/historical and a practical point of view. The chapter begins with a brief discussion of the concept of contemplation and its awareness raising effects. This discussion also outlines the difference between "contemplation" and "reflection." Reflection is then discussed from the modern era philosophical precedents.

Chapter 3, "*Framework for Reflecting on Practice*," outlines the framework in detail. As noted above, the framework has five different levels of reflection that is inclusive for ALL teachers regardless of their experience. The different levels outlined are: level 1: Philosophy; level 2: Principles; level 3: Theory; level 4: Practice; and level 5: Beyond Practice.

Chapter 4, "Philosophy," outlines and discusses how a person's basic philosophy is central to how he or she teaches because it reflects the teacher's development from childhood into pre-service teaching and beyond. This philosophy thus reflects a teacher's story and details such as personal belief development and personal value development are reflected at this level of self-development.

Chapter 5, "Principles," outlines and discusses current themes concerning the principles a teacher uses to direct his or her practice. The chapter includes an examination of a teacher's assumptions, beliefs, and conceptions of the factors that shape these.

Chapter 6, "Theory," outlines and discusses how teachers can reflect on their theory. As teachers consciously reflect at this level, they will note what theories are embedded in their general approach to their lesson planning. The chapter also explores critical incidents in detail as well as how to report and analyze cases of teachers in practice as both are a close indication of teachers' theory.

Chapter 7, "Practice," outlines and discusses what actually occurs in a teacher's practice and why and how reflecting on classroom practices are an integral part of the overall framework presented in this book. The chapter outlines how teachers can engage in classroom observations, record (audio and/or video), and transcribe their lessons as well as make use of action research projects to reflect on their practice.

Chapter 8, "Beyond Practice," encourages the teacher to go beyond the classroom and examines sociocultural, moral, and emotional impacts of reflecting on practice. After discussing the concept of critical reflection, the chapter outlines how teachers can engage in critical reflection through dialogue with other teachers in teacher reflection groups.

Chapter 9, "Navigating the Framework" outlines and discusses how teachers with different levels of experience can navigate and apply the framework in a holistic manner from whatever perspective they think will further their professional development aims as teachers of English to speakers of other languages. The chapter also outlines and discusses examples of teachers at different stages of their careers as they attempt to apply the model to their professional development needs.

Distinctive Features of the Book

The book is written in a clear and accessible style and assumes no previous background in language teacher education or reflection. Native speaker teachers and non-native speaker teachers alike will be able to interact with the contents of the book because of its accessible writing style and comprehensible vocabulary.

Regardless of which stage/level they begin their reflections, throughout each chapter (with the exception of the introductory chapter 1) there is a **Reflective Moment** where teachers can stop for a moment or two to consider some reflective questions related to the section that was just presented that may be of interest to them. As this is a book that attempts to promote reflective practice, I think such moments may be important for teachers to step back and reflect on their connections to the material and how they would consider some of the ideas that are presented. I am sure, though, that some teachers may become overwhelmed if they try to answer all of the questions (unless they are in a teacher education program and may be required to answer), so I would suggest a judicious amount of picking and choosing those questions that may be of most interest and concern rather than trying to answer them all. I attempted to provide a wide range of questions to suit all types of readers, so please decide which ones are of most interest to your particular context. It is possible also to first read each chapter and then decide which questions are of interest, or if you are really busy, just read the chapter and when you have time you can return later and consider these reflective moments.

In addition, most of the chapters have a concluding section followed by a section called **Chapter Reflections** that provide further ideas related to the chapter for teachers to reflect on. For each of the chapter reflections (and **Reflective Moments**) readers may want to consider writing their reflections and/or discussing their reflections with a peer or peers or a group of teachers. If they are considering writing their answers first, readers may want to begin their own reflections through writing before reading about the details of the framework that are explained in the remaining chapters of this book, so it may be an opportune time to begin writing about practice from this point in a teaching journal (see Farrell, 2013). Writing in a journal of some sort (it can be a notebook with a pen or word processed on a computer) can help language teachers raise questions, reflect, and analyze what they do both inside and outside the classroom because, as I have previously written, it is the very act of writing that has a built-in reflective mechanism (one of delay) that helps teachers to step back for a moment and consciously explore what they have written about their practice.

Readership

Given that the *Framework for Reflecting on Practice* was designed for all second language teachers regardless of their teaching experiences, this book is suitable for pre-service teachers in training, novice teachers, and very experienced teachers. For example, students taking CELTA and DELTA courses, and graduate courses in Applied Linguistics/TESOL such as certificate and MA courses can use the framework to reflect on their foundational theories and their practice and beyond practice. In addition, practicing classroom language teachers at all levels of experience from novice teachers to more experienced teachers can also use the framework to reflect on their practice. Experienced teachers, too, either enrolled in in-service professional development programs or interested in reflecting alone, with a colleague, peer, critical friend, or with a group of teachers can use the framework to reflect on their practice.

This book is also suitable for program administrators and supervisors who are responsible for providing professional development opportunities for novice and experienced teachers. Administrators can ask their novice teachers to read this book so that they can be better prepared for their (novice teacher) needs during this important first year. In addition, many teachers can become disillusioned after years of experience and so it is in the interests of administrators to have a deep knowledge of various aspects of reflective practice they can encourage their teachers to undertake so that they can remain committed to their practice.

I wish you a pleasant reflective journey with the contents of this book.

1

GETTING INTO REFLECTIVE PRACTICE

Introduction

One of the buzzwords in the field of education over the past 20 years or so that has taken hold and become part of nearly every description of teacher education or development programs is "reflection" or "reflective practice." If we look back further we can see that these terms can be traced to the work of the great American educator John Dewey in the 1930s, and then much later, and after a lull of sorts, again by his student Donald Schön in the early 1980s. I will say up front that these two scholars have influenced much of my work on reflective practice over the past 35 years or so as will be evident when you read this introduction and the chapters that follow in this book. This introductory chapter sets the scene for the remainder of the book and shows how I got into the area of reflective practice and how the framework that I present in the book developed from more than 35 years of my work on the concept of reflective practice.

Getting into Reflective Practice

Reflective practice entered my professional life very early and stealthily, and of course at the time I was not familiar with the term. One morning in 1977 as a teacher-learner on my teaching practice assignment in a high school in Dublin, Ireland I was teaching a business English class to junior high school students and in my fourth week or so during one class a student suddenly shouted out: "Teacher you are stupid!" I was astonished as I had no idea at that moment how to respond. Although I was in shock for a few moments, I remember that I said to the boy that he could and should not say this to me, his teacher or any teacher, and that he should write a letter of apology to me before I would let him back to my class. I then asked him to leave for the remainder of that lesson. Just before class on the following day he handed me a letter which he said he wrote as an apology. In that letter (which I still have today) he gave the following reason for saying what he had the previous day: "Teacher, I called you stupid because you were stupid because you gave us the same homework the day before and that is why you are stupid."

When I read that note I realized that he was correct as I had mistakenly given the class the same homework in the previous class. I also realized that even though we may think that our students may not be listening to their teachers, in fact, they are. Unfortunately, the student who made the statement was actually deemed a "problem" student by his regular teachers, in that he was always at the center of any class activity that the teachers had difficulty controlling; however, I always had a good relationship with him, probably because he reminded me of when I was a student at his age. I never forgot this "critical incident" and now after many years working within the topic of reflective practice, I realize it was my first intro-duction to Schön's (1983) reflection-in-action (my immediate response to the student's statement) and reflecting-on-action (my later responses). Over the years I have had many more occasions where I have experienced both reflection-in-action moments and reflection-on-action examples in different classrooms, con-texts, and countries but it was that early classroom example that has stayed with me for many years although I had no real understanding of its true meaning until I began to read Schön's (1983) seminal work on reflective practice.

About this time too in my own professional life (I was teaching English as a foreign language (EFL) in a university in Seoul, South Korea) I became very interested in my own teaching and I remember one day in a class wondering what was really happening during my lessons and how was it possible to know. Thus I became more and more interested in reflecting on what I was doing, how and why I was doing it, and so I began to read widely about how I could explore my own practice. I also decided to reflect formally and entered a doctoral program of which I have written about recently (Farrell, 2013). During my PhD studies I was again drawn to the whole concept of reflective practice and began to formalize my explorations of this fascinating concept and indeed have since spent my whole professional career investigating this concept of reflective practice within second language education. Now of course the term has become very popular (and almost mandatory) in many pre-service teacher education programs and in-service pro-fessional development programs worldwide. It seems that everyone has jumped on the bandwagon of reflective practice, and as Tabachnick and Zeichner (2002: 13) have noted, "there is not a single teacher educator who would say that he or she is not concerned about preparing teachers who are reflective."

However, I hope the contents of this book show that reflective practice is not another bandwagon term within the field of second language education even though some have said that the concept has lost some of its sharpness over these years. Yes, most teacher educators believe that some form of reflection is desirable, but they still do not agree on its definition or what it means to be "reflective." Indeed, Tabachnick and Zeichner (2002: 13–14) have noted, "the criteria that have been attached to reflective practice are so diverse" that we do not know what it is teachers should be reflecting on, or "the kinds of criteria that should come into play during the process of reflection." One of the reasons for this confusion is that there has been a hodgepodge of definitions, activities, strategies, and approaches to reflection presented both in the fields of education and second language education and there has been no consistency within any of these approaches or models that teachers, regardless of their experience, can apply to their everyday professional practice (see Chapter 1 for a detailed discussion on this). However, in *Promoting Teacher Reflection in Second-Language Education: A Framework for TESOL Professionals*, I provide a comprehensive framework that brings reflective practice together for teachers at all levels of teaching experience.

I have really been exploring this possibility of an overall reflective practice framework for over 35 years while teaching in Ireland, South Korea, Singapore, USA, and Canada. During this time I have read a lot of literature on reflective practice but as I mentioned above, I keep returning to the work of two scholars that have influenced and continue to influence my work: John Dewey and Donald Schön. I realize that I am attracted to their work because they were very pragmatic in their approaches so that they could help practicing teachers on the frontlines rather than impress academics; given my early background as a teacher in Ireland and an EFL teacher in Korea, I am still firmly connected to the reality of life in the classroom rather than the research lab. However, I do not see reflective practice as another form of navel gazing for teachers and like Dewey I consider reflective practice to be a form of systematic inquiry or evidence-based reflective practice which I also believe in and is the core of much of what is presented in this book. I was also attracted to the pragmatic work of Donald Schön (who wrote his dissertation on Dewey's Theory of Inquiry), and especially his concept of reflection-in-action, or reflecting while you are teaching. Dewey's and Schön's legacies are important because they moved the concept of reflection far beyond everyday simple wonderings about a situation (or mulling over something without taking action) to a more rigorous form of reflective thinking whereby a teacher systematically investigates a perceived problem in order to discover a workable solution over time.

Early Framework

I made some early attempts to develop some kind of model or framework for reflecting on practice that would encompass the work of both Dewey and Schön, where teachers are encouraged to engage in evidence-based reflective practice (e.g., see Farrell, 2004). At that time my model emphasized the idea that practicing teachers would be better able to "locate themselves within their profession and start to take more responsibility for shaping their practice" (Farrell, 2004: 6). This framework (Farrell, 2004) of reflective teaching is composed of five components: (a) a range of opportunities and activities, (b) ground rules, (c) provision for four different times or categories of reflection, (d) external input, and (e) trust. The most important aspect of this framework is to give teachers the opportunity to reflect, and I believe it is still useful today. While I have used this framework successfully and very recently with experienced language teachers in a teacher reflection group in Canada (see Farrell, 2014), and it is still useful for teachers wishing to reflect on their practice, I believe it is still too general in its overall approach and only covers three ways of reflecting on practice: group discussions, classroom observations, and written reflections. In addition, this framework may be somewhat challenging for novice teachers to enact unless they have mentors to help them. So I was looking to develop a framework that provided more depth to reflection and that included all teachers regardless of their teaching experience (see Chapter 1 for more on this model).

Developing a New Framework

I re-read and reflected on both Dewey's and Schön's work recently as well as other scholars and revisited my early framework of reflection following my work with three experienced Canadian ESL teachers (Farrell, 2014) to see if I could develop an overall framework of reflective practice for TESOL professionals. I also re-examined other different models and frameworks to see if these held any useful points for me to consider. For example, one early model, which I call the "Loop Model" by Donald Schön and Chris Argyris, developed the notion of single-loop and double-loop learning (see Argyris and Schön, 1974). Without getting into too much detail here it was the "looping" back and forth (or framing and reframing a problem) that attracted me again to this model. I also re-read Schön's work where he distinguished between technical rationality and tacit knowledge or the theory-practice gap. Schön (1983) was interested in how professionals "know" through their practice because he was convinced they know more about their practice than they can articulate. As Schön (1983: vii) noted: "We are in need of inquiry into the epistemology of practice. What is the kind of knowing in which competent practitioners engage? How is professional knowing like and unlike the kinds of knowing in academic textbooks, scientific papers and journals?" Schön, like Dewey, maintained that reflection begins in professional practice, some of which may be "messy" and confusing and so even though teachers may have obtained their subject matter knowledge—their theoretical knowledge (technical rationality)—this does not explain what actual classroom practice is because teachers obtain their tacit knowledge from these real-classroom experiences. As such, teachers must engage in reflection-in-action (thinking on their feet) as well as reflection-on-action (after the class) and these should be documented in some manner so that they can also help teachers to reflect-for-action (see Farrell, 2004). As Stanley (1998: 585) has noted, these entail what "reflective practitioners do when they look at their work in the moment (reflect-in-action) or in retrospect (reflect-on-action) in order to examine the reasons and beliefs underlying their actions and generate alternative actions for the future."

One further model/framework that also influenced the development of the framework presented in this book is Shapiro and Reiff's (1993) model from the field of psychology. Shapiro and Reiff (1993) called their model, reflective inquiry on practice (or RIP) and it divided the process of reflection into five basic levels—philosophy, basic theory, theory of technique, technique, and moves. Although this model was developed mostly for the purposes of interviewing experienced practitioners (in a retrospective analysis type discussion) interested in analyzing their practice, and it does not address the important issue of critical reflection, nevertheless, I like their idea of different stages or levels of reflection and so decided to incorporate something similar into my new *Framework for Reflecting on Practice* for language teachers. The five different stages or levels of the new framework presented in this book are: Philosophy; Principles; Theory; Practice; and Beyond Practice. Chapter 3 outlines and discusses this framework in more detail.

Conclusion

In this introductory chapter I have attempted to map out where and how I developed the new *Framework for Reflecting on Practice* developed from my many years of work with the concept of reflective practice. This new framework, which consists of five stages/levels of reflection that starts with reflecting on philosophy and then moves to principles, theory, practice, and beyond practice, can be used by all language teachers regardless of their level of teaching experience. This makes it unique in our field because to my knowledge no such overall framework exists. In addition, teachers are encouraged to reflect beyond practice or beyond their classroom, a much neglected aspect of reflecting on practice in second language education. The remaining chapters explain the concept of reflection (and contemplation), the framework, and how the framework can be navigated by all teachers.

2

CONTEMPLATION AND REFLECTION

Introduction

The term "reflection" comes from the Latin word "reflectere" and means "to bend back" (Valli, 1997: 67) or to look back and become more aware of a past event or issue. Some teachers may think of reflection as common sense thinking in that most people tend to think about what they do, such as teachers thinking about what they want to do before a class, and/or thinking about how a lesson went. Some scholars have suggested that this is not real reflective practice as it does not involve any systematic reflections in any ordered manner and as such should not be included with the concept of reflective practice. Although, I agree that this type of "common sense" reflection tends to be vague, and not very organized, I believe it can be an important prerequisite to the more disciplined and ordered reflection that is more evidence-based and is presented in this book. I believe that teachers can actually develop their "common sense reflections" a bit more and enter into "contemplative reflective practice" in its more developed stage. In this chapter I introduce the idea of contemplation as an awareness raising reflective tool and in Chapter 3 (under stage/level 1 of the framework, *philosophy*) I discuss "contemplative reflective practice" in more detail. In this chapter I also outline and discuss definitions, approaches, purposes, and models or frameworks of reflective practice. These deliberations then set the scene for the introduction to the framework for reflective practice (see Chapter 3) that will best facilitate the development of reflection for teachers at all levels of experience.

Contemplation

The concept of contemplation and its awareness raising effects has long been a part of great religions and philosophical studies. For example, in Buddhism practitioners are encouraged to become more mindful of the "here-and-now," and Existentialism encourages contemplation of the inevitable mortality of human beings. Such contemplations place individuals at the center of the contemplative process but without trying to take any control or intervention of the contemplations so that they become more aware of their surroundings in a more mindful way. In order to engage in such a contemplative process as Miller (1994: 3) explains, means possessing a "radical openness in which the individual does not try to control what is happening." Such contemplations mean being able to consciously observe the self in the present moment simply by paying "careful attention and quiet wonder," (Buchman, 1989: 39) without any intervention so that we can become more aware of who we are as human beings.

I believe that such contemplation can be a precursor to more systematic and evidence-based reflective practice because it can help teachers become more aware of themselves as human beings first. I also believe that in order to gain such knowledge of who we are and how we interact with the world we need to engage in contemplation because we usually hold such tacit knowledge in our subconscious. As Polanyi (1967: 4) has noted, much of our knowledge is difficult to put into words and "we know more than we can tell." Thus using Polanyi's (1962, 1967) views on tacit knowledge we can say that contemplation could be a pre-logical phase of knowing. For example, Polanyi (1962: 54) observed that when a person (in any field) carries out a skillful performance, this performance includes "actions, recognitions, and judgments which we know how to carry out spontaneously; we do not have to think about them prior to or during" the performance. The person carrying out the performance may be unaware of ever having learned the skill or how he or she became skilled in the first place. He or she just performs. In fact, it is like recognizing a face in a crowd without being able to list the features of that face in words or as Polanyi (1967: 5) says: "We recognize the moods of the human face, without being able to tell, except quite vaguely, by what signs we know it." I call this "contemplative reflective practice" (see Chapter 3 for more details) and a necessary pre-logical phase of "reflection" so that we can become more aware of who we are as human beings. For language teachers awareness of ourselves as human beings is a necessary starting point in any teacher reflections because as Knezedivc (2001:10) has indicated, we should become aware of "who we are" before reflecting on "what we do."

Reflective Moment

- Are you a contemplative person by nature?
- How has contemplating affected your work?
- Do you think reflecting is the same as contemplating?
- How would you define reflection and reflective practice (compare your answer to what you read in the next section and the reflective moment that follows)?

Reflection

As mentioned above there is a difference between contemplation and reflection. Whereas both lead to more self-awareness, when contemplating there is no distinction between the thinker and the subject he or she is thinking about (an object) because they are one. However, when engaging in reflection there is such a distinction because there is a subject thinking consciously about something (an object) (Miller, 1994). So reflection generally means conscious thinking about what we are doing and why we are doing it. Within the field of education many different terms have been used to refer to reflection and reflective practice and include many of the following key words (my italics) to define its focus; it is seen as a *process* of *recognizing, examining, deliberating over* the *impact* and *implications* of one's *beliefs, experiences, attitudes, knowledge,* and *values* on *classroom practices* (Copeland et al., 1993; Bailey, 2010; Farrell, 1999b, 2012, 2013; Hatton and Smith, 1995; Stanley, 1998). As Jay and Johnson (2002: 76) suggest: "Reflection is a process, both individual and collaborative, involving experience and uncertainty. It is comprised of identifying questions and key elements of a matter that has emerged as significant, then taking one's thoughts into dialogue with oneself and with others."

Within the field of second language education reflective practice has emerged as an approach where teachers actively collect data about their teaching beliefs and practices and then reflect on the data in order to direct future teaching decisions (Bailey, 2010; Farrell, 2010, 2012; Perfecto, 2008). This evidence-based approach to reflection encourages teachers to avoid making instructional decisions based on impulse or routine; rather, teachers are now encouraged to use the data they have obtained so that they can make more informed decisions about their practice (Chien, 2013; Farrell, 2014; Perfecto, 2008). Richards' and Lockhart's (1994: 1) definition summarizes this evidence-based reflective approach as they encourage teachers to "collect data about their teaching, examine their attitudes, beliefs, assumptions, and teaching practices, and use the information obtained as a basis for critical reflection about teaching."

So far I have talked about reflection in a technical manner in that it is focused on examining classroom events and teaching routines. However, classroom lessons do not occur in a vacuum (although it may seem so because the door is usually closed) and there is nothing neutral about our practices, so reflective practice should also include a close critical examination of the cultural, social, and political setting where our teaching takes place (Smith, 2011). This is called critical reflection and as Brookfield (1995: 8) has noted, such reflection has two purposes: "(1) to understand how considerations of power undergird, frame and distort educational processes and interactions. (2) To question assumptions and practices that seem to make our teaching lives easier but actually work against or own best long term interests." Although largely ignored within TESOL until very recently scholars such as Graham Crooks have called for a more critical second language pedagogy that includes "teaching for social justice, in ways that support the development of active, engaged citizens who . . . will be prepared to seek out solution to the problems they define and encounter, and take action accordingly" (Crooks, 2013: 8). The *Framework for Reflecting on Practice* that I present in this book includes coverage of critical reflection in what I call reflecting *beyond practice* (see Chapter 8).

Reflective Moment

- Read the following different definitions of reflective practice. What is your understanding of these and which one(s) do you subscribe to and why?
  Ghaye and Ghaye (1998: 16): "Reflective practice is a way to improve our thinking about what we do, the act of teaching and learning itself, and the contexts in which teaching and learning take place."
  Cruickshank and Applegate (1981: 553): "Reflection helps teachers to think about what happened, why it happened, and what else could have been done to reach their goals."
  Hatton and Smith (1995: 35): "Reflection is more than constructive self-criticism of one's actions with a view to improvement"; it "implies the acceptance of a particular ideology."
  Loughran (2002: 34): "Reflective practice is a meaningful way of approaching learning and teaching so that a better understanding of teaching, and teaching about teaching, might develop."

Levels of Reflection

Many scholars suggest that it is difficult to define reflective practice because it can mean different things to different people (e.g., see **Reflective Moment** above); however there is agreement on three basic different levels of reflection (although some may use different terminology to explain them) that teachers can work from (e.g., Farrell, 2004, 2007a; Jay and Johnson, 2002; Larrivee, 2008; Van Manen, 1977). These three levels are called: *descriptive* (focus on teacher skills), *conceptual* (the rationale for practice) and *critical* (examination of socio-political and moral and ethical results of practice—see critical pedagogy above). Jay and Johnson (2002: 77–9) have neatly summarized the three levels outlined above although they use slightly different terminology for the second level (they call it *comparative reflection*) as follows.

- *Descriptive reflection* involves describing a situation or problem.
- *Comparative reflection* involves thinking about the situation for reflection from different perspectives. Teachers try to solve the problem while also questioning their values and beliefs.
- *Critical reflection* involves teachers looking at all the different perspectives of a situation/problem and all of the players involved: teachers, students, the school and the community.

The first level, *descriptive reflection*, involves some kind of descriptions of practice at its very basis or the answer to the question of "what do I do?" and "How do I do it?" The next basic level, *conceptual* or *comparative reflection*, asks "why do you do it?" and in order to answer, teachers must conceptualize their practice and compare what they do with what others do. These two levels in themselves, as I mentioned above, do not constitute *critical reflection* because this third level means going beyond one's practice and examining the context outside the classroom and encompasses reflecting on the social, political, ethical, and moral aspects of practice (see Chapter 8 for more on this). Some scholars have suggested that critical reflection is what each teacher should strive to reach because it is the most important level of reflection. I am not sure I would go that far because I believe that the other introductory levels of reflection, descriptive and conceptual, are also very important levels of reflection for many teachers, but especially for novice teachers who are still developing during their teacher preparation courses and in their first years of teaching (Farrell 2007b). I believe each teacher can decide when he or she is ready to move from one level to another. All levels are covered in the *Framework for Reflecting on Practice* presented in this book.

Reflective Moment

- What is your understanding of the three different levels of reflection (descriptive, conceptual, and critical) discussed in the section above?
- What do you think *your* level of reflection is: descriptive, conceptual, or critical?
- Which level should a teacher reflect at and why?
- *Check your level*: although the following questions are not very scientific they will nonetheless get you started on considering what level of reflection you may be at and this will help facilitate a discussion on what level you want to reflect at (adapted from Taggart and Wilson, 1998). Read the statements below and for each statement, circle the number of the indicator that best reflects your agreement and give yourself points for each answer as follows: *4 = Almost always*; *3 = Regularly*; *2 = Situational*; *1 = Seldom*

I can identify a problem or puzzle related to my practice	4 3 2 1
I analyze a problem/puzzle based upon the needs of the student	4 3 2 1
I seek evidence which supports or refutes my decision (in # 2)	4 3 2 1
I view problems/puzzles in an ethical context	4 3 2 1
I use an organized approach to solving problems/puzzles	4 3 2 1
I am intuitive in making judgments	4 3 2 1
I creatively interpret problems/puzzles	4 3 2 1
My actions vary with the context of the problem/puzzle	4 3 2 1
I feel most comfortable with a set routine	4 3 2 1
I have strong commitment to values related to my practice	4 3 2 1
I am responsive to the educational needs of my students	4 3 2 1

I review my personal aims and actions related to my practice   4 3 2 1
I am flexible in my thinking related to my practice   4 3 2 1
I have a questioning nature   4 3 2 1
I welcome peer review of my professional actions   4 3 2 1
I use innovative ideas in my lessons   4 3 2 1
My teaching focus is on my lesson objectives   4 3 2 1
There is no best approach to teaching   4 3 2 1
I have the skills necessary to be a successful teacher   4 3 2 1
I have the content necessary to be a successful teacher   4 3 2 1
I consciously modify my teaching to meet my students' needs   4 3 2 1
I complete tasks adequately   4 3 2 1
I understand concepts, procedures, and skills related to practice   4 3 2 1
I consider the social implications of my practice   4 3 2 1
I set long-term teaching goals   4 3 2 1
I self-monitor my teaching   4 3 2 1
I evaluate my teaching effectiveness   4 3 2 1
My students usually meet my instructional objectives   4 3 2 1
I write about my practice regularly   4 3 2 1
I engage in action research   4 3 2 1

Scoring Procedures: Add up all the circled numbers: Total_____
What level was most evident? *Descriptive = Below 75; Conceptual = 75 to 104; Critical = 105 to 120.*

o   What attributes do you consider to be most indicative of a reflective practitioner?
o   Write examples of each statement above: create possible examples or actions derived from possession of each statement.
o   What level should teachers reflect at?

Approaches to Reflection

Similar to the situation of all the different definitions of reflective practice as discussed above, it will not be surprising to note the many different approaches to reflective practice that exist and the many different terms that have been used by scholars to describe these different approaches. Although some of the terms have been in existence since its emergence in the 1970s (e.g., Schön, 1983, 1987; Van Manen, 1977), they have also been used in more recent literature within the field of second language education summarized as follows:

• *Technical rationality*: Examining the use of skills and immediate behaviors in teaching with an established research and theory base (Chien, 2013).
• *Reflection-in-action*: Dealing with on-the-spot professional problems as they occur. This mode of reflection involves a reflective conversation where the practitioner is listening to the "situations' backtalk" and thus engages in an

interactive process of problem setting rather than problem solving (Chien, 2013; Farrell, 2014; Yang, 2009).

- *Reflection-on-action*: Recalling one's teaching after the class. This "recollective" mode of reflection involves the teacher exploring reasons for his or her actions and behaviors in class (Chien, 2013; Farrell, 2010, 2012; Majid, 2008; Yang, 2009).
- *Reflection-for-action*: Proactive thinking in order to guide future action as the teacher anticipates what may happen in class and can be based on the results of the previous modes of reflection (Chien, 2013; Farrell, 2013).
- *Action research*: Self-reflective inquiry by participants in social settings to improve classroom practice and can involve reflection or critical reflection outside the classroom (Chien, 2013; Crooks, 2013).

Discussions on the above approaches to reflective practice have also included the debate about the various phases connected to reflective practice such as (again interested readers with time may want to look up the various citations for more detailed explanations of each one):

1. *Problem identification*: A doubtful situation is understood to be problematic (Farrell, 2012; Josten, 2011).
2. *Generating solutions*: Possible solutions to the problem are generated (Farrell, 2012; Burton, 2009).
3. *Testing solutions*: The refined idea is reached, and the testing of this refined hypothesis takes place; the testing can be by overt action or in thought (Bailey, 2010; Farrell, 2010, 2012; Perfecto, 2008).
4. *Learning from reflecting*: The reflective process leads to an enhancement of the teacher's understanding used to give meaning to the professional context in which the problem was identified (Bailey, 2010; Farrell, 2010, 2012; Chien, 2013).

Summarizing many of the above phases, Loughran (2002: 42) has noted that for reflective practice to be effective it must be: "drawn from the ability to frame and reframe the practice setting, to develop and respond to this framing through action so that the practitioner's wisdom-in-action is enhanced, and, as a particular outcome, articulation of professional knowledge is encouraged." In addition, Dewey (1933) has noted that although approaches to reflection are mainly cognitive, to be effective they must also be accompanied by a set of attitudes to make the reflection truly meaningful. He suggested that teachers who want to be considered truly reflective must possess (at least) three characteristics (or attitudes). They must be *open-minded, responsible* and *wholehearted*. Teachers must be *open-minded* with an active desire to listen to more than one side of an issue and then to admit they could be wrong and as a result must be willing to change a belief or practice. Teachers must be *responsible* by making careful consideration of the consequences to which an action leads because all teachers' actions impact the students, the community, and the society at large. In addition, teachers must be *wholehearted* in their approach to reflective practice to continually review their beliefs and actions, and to seek every opportunity to continue to learn and develop themselves as human beings and teachers. As a result, for teachers to maintain such a reflective disposition, they must continue to reflect-*in-on-for*-action throughout their careers.

Reflective Moment

* How do you think reflection-in-action, reflection-on-action, reflection-for-action and action research are linked?
* What is the difference between problem solving and problem posing?
* Do you agree with Dewey's three essential attitudes associated with reflective practice and what levels of each do you possess? Can you think of other desirable characteristics or dispositions a reflective practitioner should possess?

Purposes of Reflection

An early and very noble, all-encompassing purpose of reflective practice was posited by Argyris and Schön (1974) that I think is still relevant today: they maintained that the purpose of reflection is for the creation of a world that more faithfully reflects its beliefs and values. This to me is the true essence of reflective practice in all the disciplines because it holds people accountable for their actions as well as their non-actions be they teachers, physicians, scientists, nurses, immigration officers, or garbage collectors. We are who we want to be and our actions should reflect who we are. Here are 10 more purposes of engaging in reflective practice that come from many different disciplines, such as education and medicine, which have been adapted for TESOL professionals, the focus of this book.

1. Develop individual theories of TESOL and thus become generators rather than consumers of knowledge.
2. After describing practice, reflection can advance theories of TESOL at the conceptual level and this can in turn lead to changes at professional, social, and political levels.
3. Allow for a greater integration of theory and practice in TESOL.
4. Enable TESOL teachers to explore their beliefs and practice through evidence-based reflective practice as this can lead to an acceptance of professional responsibility for practice.
5. Allow for any correction of distortions and errors in beliefs related to practice so that TESOL teachers can recognize and discontinue practices not in the best interests of their students.
6. Allow for the identification, description, and resolution of practical problems through evidence-based reflective practice.

7. Enhance TESOL teachers' self-esteem and self-confidence through reflective practice.
8. Heighten the visibility of TESOL teachers in the profession through evidence-based reflective practice so that others can also realize the complexity of teaching English to speakers of other languages.
9. Support TESOL teachers to explore and understand the nature and boundaries of their roles as TESOL professionals.
10. Develop resourcefulness and resilience required to face future challenges and changes in profession.

Reflective Moment

• For what purposes do you use or have you used reflection in your work (and in your life)?
• Discuss the 10 purposes outlined above in terms of TESOL professionals, reflecting on practice, and rank them in order of importance for you.
• Can you add more purposes?

Models of Reflection

Many different models, frameworks, and strategies have been used to promote reflection. Most, if not all, of the models have their uses for teachers but because there are so many different models and frameworks in existence, and for brevity of discussion, I only outline and describe those main models and frameworks that have influenced my thoughts on reflective practice and more importantly have had an influence on the development of the *Framework for Reflecting on Practice* that I present in this book (see Chapter 3).

While I acknowledge the many different models of frameworks for reflecting on practice that have contributed to our current understandings of reflective practice, John Dewey's (1933) model of *reflective inquiry* has had a large (probably the largest) impact on my work in reflective practice throughout the past 35 years. Dewey (1933) maintained that when teachers want to engage in reflective practice, one of the most important things they should first do is slow down the interval between thought and action. This means not jumping to conclusions before one has had a chance to examine an issue or problem, and he said this can be accomplished by following five main phases of reflective inquiry:

1. *Suggestion*: A doubtful situation is understood to be problematic, and some vague suggestions are considered as possible solutions. For example, in language teaching (or any field really) we may have noted that our students make many mistakes in grammar while writing. However, at this stage we try

to avoid making any judgments and we look for some alternatives rather than just blaming our students. Perhaps it has something to do with our teaching or the curriculum: we do not know yet.

2. *Intellectualization*: The difficulty or perplexity of the problem that has been felt (directly experienced) is intellectualized into a problem to be solved. Here we move from a problem felt to a problem to be solved so we begin to refine the problem by asking a question. For example, I now begin to ask if the problem has something to do with my grammar corrections.

3. *Guiding idea*: One suggestion after another is used as a leading idea, or hypothesis; the initial suggestion can be used as a working hypothesis to initiate and guide observation and other operations in the collection of factual material. We now begin to look at some details such as what do I do as a teacher when correcting so I examine students' papers with my grammar corrections and review the literature on grammar correction, which says teachers should not correct all grammar mistakes. As a result I decide it must be something to do with my corrections so I have to change them.

4. *Reasoning*: Reasoning links present and past ideas and helps elaborate the supposition that reflective inquiry has reached, or the mental elaboration of the idea or supposition as an idea or supposition. So through reasoning I decide to implement selective grammar corrections but I am not sure yet if this will work.

5. *Hypothesis testing*: The refined idea is reached, and the testing of this refined hypothesis takes place; the testing can be by overt action or in thought (imaginative action). I begin now to test and monitor my selective grammar corrections by action and observation in practice. If successful, then I can draw strong positive conclusions to my solutions. If this fails, then I must try some other solution and see what may happen.

The reflective inquiry cycle outlined above is very similar to action research procedures that have been proposed in general education and in TESOL. My own work in reflective practice has been influenced by this reflective inquiry cycle because it encourages evidence-based reflective practice. This reflective inquiry cycle has influenced the work of other scholars over the years, who have since built on this model. For example, Boud et al. (1985) have suggested a cyclical model with three broader categories of reflective thought (experience, reflection, and outcome) that emphasize emotion as an element of reflective practice. In addition, Zeichner and Liston (1996: 24) also returned to Dewey's (1933) original ideas when they distinguished between routine action and reflective action and suggested that, for teachers, "routine action is guided primarily by tradition, external authority and circumstance" whereas reflective action "entails the active, persistent and careful consideration of any belief or supposed form of knowledge." Zeichner and Liston's (1996: 44–7) framework is also a precursor to many similar models that appeared later in the literature on reflective practice and their model consists of five dimensions or phases of reflection:

1. *Rapid reaction*: Something happens and a teacher acts instinctively. The teacher is immediate in reflection and action. This corresponds to immediate reflection-in-action.
2. *Repair*: The teacher pauses for thought about what happened. May try to repair the situation. This is more thoughtful reflection-in-action than in phase 1.
3. *Review*: The teacher takes time out (hours or days) to reassess the situation. This is a form of delayed and casual reflection-on-action.
4. *Research*: A teacher researches the situation in all its forms (systematic). This is more systematic and deliberative reflection-on-action.
5. *Re-theorize/research*: The teacher rethinks the situation in light of what he or she has discovered during the previous four phases of reflection and engages in more long-term reflection while looking at theories already in place and what others have done.

Another early but very influential model of reflective practice that is sometimes forgotten in the literature these days was developed by Kolb and Fry (1975). They initially mapped out four phases of reflection: (1) experience, (2) reflective observation, (3) abstract conceptualization, and (4) active experimentation. Many authors and scholars within the field of education have since built on and developed this reflective model to promote reflective practice. For example, when developing his ALACT (A = Action; L = Looking; A = Awareness; C = Creating; T = Trial) model of reflective practice, Korthagen (1985) adapted Kolb and Fry's (1975) model and this newer version of the model has been used since then in many teacher education programs. The ALACT model of reflection consists of five phases: (1) Action, (2) Looking back on the action, (3) Awareness of essential aspects, (4) Creating alternative methods of action, and (5) Trial, which itself is a new action and thus the starting point of a new cycle. In addition, Kolb's (1984) work on experiential learning and understanding learning styles through reflective observation is also an influence on the concept of reflective inquiry discussed in this book.

My own early framework for reflecting on practice (Farrell, 2004, 2007a), as I mentioned in the introduction to the book, has also influenced the development of the new framework I present in this book. My early framework attempted to articulate an overall approach to reflecting on practice, mostly for experienced teachers, which was grounded in their own classroom practices (Farrell, 2004). This framework consists of five interconnected dimensions or stages of reflection as follows:

1. Provide different opportunities for teachers to reflect through a range of activities.
2. Build ground rules into the process and into each activity.

3. Make provisions for four different categories of time (individual, activity, development, reflection).
4. Provide external input for enriched reflection.
5. Provide for low affective states.

The framework is still in use and is mainly for a group of teachers (mostly experienced, but novice teachers could also use it although, I would suggest with the aid of a facilitator to guide them through it) wishing to reflect on their practice rather than individual teachers. Briefly, the framework suggests that opportunities be made for teachers to reflect by providing particular tools for reflection. The main tools by which teachers can make use of these opportunities are through journaling, classroom observations, and group discussions. These strategies can be used both individually and collaboratively. By ground rules, I refer to the notion that rules for reflection are essential in order to "focus" reflections. These rules include determining who will lead group meetings, classroom observations, and how reflection will occur, and should be discussed before reflection can occur. I also proposed that teachers should have an understanding of four different kinds of time that are important for reflection: individual time describes how much time each individual in a group should spend on reflection; activity time refers to how much time is spent on the reflective activity; development time outlines the amount of time that is necessary for an individual to develop into someone who is able to reflect; and period of reflection time describes the length of time a teacher wants to reflect as a whole. The fourth component of external input involves peer-to-peer comparison by teachers as they examine the results of their reflections and connection to theories. This can be implemented through seminars and conferences. The final part of the early model discusses the importance of trust in reflective practice. It is essential for the reflective environment to be supportive and nurturing so that teachers can freely share their ideas. Within this framework, I have also suggested that reflective activities be tailored to the needs of the individual teacher (see Farrell, 2001, for a full discussion on how this can be achieved).

One final model that I present in this section, and that I already referred to in the previous chapter that has influenced the development of the framework I present in this book is the work of psychologists Shapiro and Reiff (1993). Both of these clinical psychologists were interested in developing a model of reflection that addressed the needs of experienced professionals engaged in continuing education and who wished to get a better understanding of their practices. Shapiro and Reiff (1993) considered reflective practice as an active process of examining individual practices and theories, and they called this process *Reflective Inquiry on Practice* (RIP). Their model outlined a process of reflective inquiry on practice (RIP) that was divided into specific stages or levels that began at level 1 with an examination of *philosophy* of practice (this they assumed was to be the most powerful cause of a person's practice). This was followed by level 2 reflections called *basic theory* (this they considered less influential than philosophy because they may be derived from philosophical premises). Included in their basic theory approach that Shapiro and Reiff (1993) considered relevant to practice were McGregor's (1960) Theory X and Theory Y attitudes of people's motivations in organizational settings. Level 3 reflections came next and outlined *theory of practice* that also included what they called *theory of techniques*, which they noted was embedded in a general approach to practice. This was followed by level 4 reflections called *technique*. At this level Shapiro and Reiff (1993) noted practitioners reflect on their deliberate professional behavior and this included examining their lectures, role-playing, dialogues, panel discussions, group problem-solving activities, simulations and any other activities they engaged in. Level 5, the final level of reflections, was called *interventions or moves*. They suggested that moves are behaviors that are directly observed in professional practice.

They distinguish their model from the work of Schön (1983, 1987) most notably in that they focus on reflection-on-action—that is, after the event and not in action—and they note that the reflection should take place in the context of a supportive group situation (much like my first model). However, they suggest that their framework is similar in purpose to Argyris's and Schön's (1974) reflection and double-loop learning through understanding the various relationships among and between different levels of inquiry to improve professional practice. In addition, their framework was designed exclusively to help experienced professionals that they sometimes called "experts" to engage in Kolb's (1984) reflective observation so that they could notice patterns in their practice. I was attracted to Shapiro and Reiff's (1993) framework, however, because it can be considered a form through which the process of reflection can *flow* as this gave me the idea of having different levels of reflection which move from reflecting on theories, to the craft of teaching, and beyond practice. I agree with Shapiro and Reiff (1993: 1380) when they note that we need to make our meta-theory explicit because we "really do not know the strategic questions to ask should we be interested in reflection on action or practice." The framework that I present in this book is one such model that helps teachers examine their meta-theory and, unlike Shapiro and Reiff's (1993) exclusive focus on experienced teachers, this framework can be used by any teacher regardless of his or her years of teaching experience as it is structured in a manner that accounts for particular teachers' level of teaching experiences.

Reflective Moment

- Which of the models above appeal to you and why?
- What are the differences between the different models outlined above?

- Which of the models apply to your work?
- Look at Zeichner and Liston's (1996) five dimensions of reflection. Some educators have said that teachers do not proceed beyond the first two levels. Why do you think this may be?
- How useful do you think my model of reflective practice could be for you professionally?
- Why is time (e.g., my model has four different times: *individual*: each teacher's invested time in reflection; *activity*: time spent on each activity; *development*: time it takes for individual teachers to develop as a result of reflecting on their work; *reflection*: is the period of time a teacher (and pair or group) can spend on his or her reflections) an important factor when considering reflective practice?
- Why do you think I included the idea that teachers should look externally to see what others have done? Where could teachers get this external input? What research could teachers read up on? What books and journal articles would be appropriate to read or do you read now as part of your training/ education or your professional development?
- Although Shapiro and Reiff's (1993) model of reflective inquiry on practice is somewhat complicated it nevertheless suggests that a person's values can determine their choice of theory which in turn influences implementation of practice, or moving from theory-into-practice. What is your understanding of this flow process they suggest?
- If you were to develop your own model of reflection, what would you include in this model and why?
- How would you use your model?

While examining the various definitions, approaches, purposes, and models of reflective practice above, we can begin to see that most of them suggest that reflection is best defined or described as a process and its implementation in terms of specific strategies that are applied in particular phases. Most of the models I have outlined in this chapter begin with the identification of a problem, followed by close examination where teachers are encouraged to collect data about the problem and take some kind of action and then monitor the results. Thus most models encourage reflection for generating new evidence of understanding of a problem.

Although I still find such models compelling for generating evidence-based reflective understandings of practice, no one model provides any overall application of reflecting on practice that includes all teachers, from pre-service and novice to the most experienced teachers. Indeed, most of the models assume that teachers, whatever their level of experience, can benefit from reflecting through these various phases by using particular strategies and that as a result of these structured reflections, their practice will be improved. However, teachers at different times in their careers have different needs and desires in terms of their professional development and as such some teachers may need more specific scaffolding in order to develop their ability to reflect on their practice if their reflections are going to be more than mere descriptions of what they do (see discussion of the different levels of reflection earlier in this chapter). For example, pre-service and novice teachers may need more guidance when they attempt to connect their descriptions of what they do to a theoretical framework, and further, when connecting these to broader societal issues if they want to engage in critical reflection. One framework in the field of nursing has attempted to include the stimulation of reflection from novice to advanced levels by asking three questions: What? So what? Now what? (Rolfe et al., 2011). Their three-level reflective framework for healthcare professionals is very similar to other three-level frameworks outlined in this chapter; however, they maintain that only more experienced practitioners (rather than novice practitioners) beyond the descriptive "what?" level can begin to construct a personal theory at level 2 of "so what?" and then onto level 3 reflections of the broader issues related to patient care.

While most models and frameworks have admirably provided different types of structured reflection for practitioners by offering probing questions that stimulate reflection (and all these are also included in the framework presented in this book), they have mostly guided teachers on how to tackle technical issues without looking at the person who is reflecting. In other words, many models do not look at reflective practice in any overall manner that includes the person who is reflecting as well as what the person is reflecting on. In this book I try to move the concept of reflective practice to this more holistic approach by providing an overall framework for teachers to reflect on their philosophy, beliefs, values, theories, principles, classroom practices, and beyond the classroom. To my knowledge no such comprehensive framework exists within the field of TESOL that can facilitate the development of reflective practice for all teachers regardless of their level of experience and on all aspects of our practice, including going beyond practice. Chapter 3 outlines and discusses the framework in more detail.

Conclusion

The main aim of this chapter was to give an overall view of summaries of definitions of reflective practice as well as different approaches, purposes, and models of reflective practice. The discussion suggested that no overall model or framework exists that promotes reflection for TESOL professionals at different levels of experience and so I have outlined one such overall model or framework that includes much of what already exists in many of the definitions, approaches, purposes, and models that were discussed.

Chapter Reflections

- Donald Schön (1983) maintains that reflective practice will "open an inquiry into the art and intuition of practice" (p. vii). What is your understanding of this statement?
- Zeichner and Liston (1996: 6) have suggested that the roles of a reflective teacher include the following:
  o   To examine, frame, and attempt to solve dilemmas in classroom practice.
  o   To be aware of and question the assumptions and values he/she brings to teaching.
  o   To be attentive to the institutional and cultural contexts in which he/she teaches.
  o   Takes part in curriculum development and is involved in school change efforts.
  o   Takes responsibility for his or her own professional development.
    - What is your understanding of each of these roles?
    - Try to give examples of each of these features from your recent reflections. Or outline how you incorporate each of these features in your future reflections on your practice.
- Hatton and Smith (1995: 36) see a number of "barriers which hinder the achievement of reflective approaches" stated as follows: "Reflection is seen as a more academic exercise and as such seen as 'research' and teachers cannot see the need for conducting such 'research.' Teachers need time and opportunity for development. At the moment they do not have this extra time available in most fast-paced school settings. Exposing oneself in a group of strangers (such as reflecting with other teachers) can lead to vulnerability."
  o   Which of the cautions outlined above do you agree with and why?
  o   Which of the cautions outlined above do you disagree with and why?
  o   Can you think of any other cautions that teachers should think about regarding reflective practice? List them.
- Some scholars say that if reflective practice is going to have any impact, it should be a voluntary and intentional undertaking as a means of improving professional practice and classroom outcomes (Josten, 2011; Majid, 2008; Perfecto, 2008; Smith, 2011). What is your opinion of this idea?
- Do you think pre-service and novice teachers can engage in meaningful reflective practice given that they do not have much classroom teaching experience (if any)?
- If not, why not? If yes, what approach to reflective practice (from the discussion above) should pre-service teachers and novice teachers engage in and why?

3

FRAMEWORK FOR REFLECTING ON PRACTICE

Introduction

Previously I have noted that although there are many different models, frameworks, and strategies for reflection, language teachers, whether novice or experienced, still do not have any overall framework to guide their reflections on practice. I have also explained that reflective practice can include contemplations but that it is really evidenced-based where teachers obtain information (data) about their practice and use the information (data) to make informed decisions about their practice and beyond their practice. The framework presented in this chapter embraces evidence-based reflective practice. In this way teachers can become more aware not only of their actions but also the origins, meanings and impact of such actions far beyond the classroom. They can access these by examining the philosophy, principles, and theory associated with their practice and the results of these reflections can be used as a basis for further evaluation and decision making when planning any future actions in and beyond the classroom. The chapter begins with a short discussion of the development of the framework and then outlines and discusses the *Framework for Reflecting on Practice* in more detail.

Framework for Reflecting on Practice

Figure 3.1 illustrates the *Framework for Reflecting on Practice*. The framework has five different stages/levels of reflection: *Philosophy, Principles, Theory, Practice,* and *Beyond Practice*. Although each of the five stages/levels within the framework are treated separately readers should realize these are not isolated stages or levels of reflection as all are linked and each stage or level builds on the other (see two-way arrows) and all stages must be considered as a whole to give us a holistic reflective practice experience.

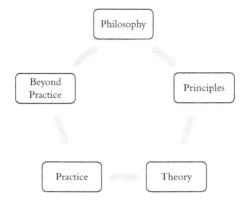

FIGURE 3.1 *Framework for Reflecting on Practice*

The framework not only addresses each level from a theoretical perspective but also asks probing questions and outlines strategies to stimulate reflection. Throughout the reflective process, teachers are encouraged not only to describe but also to examine and challenge embedded assumptions at each level so that they can use the framework as a lens through which they can view their professional (and even personal) worlds, and what has shaped their professional lives as they become more aware of their philosophy, principles, theories, practices, and how these impact issues inside and beyond the classroom. I outline and discuss each stage/level separately so teachers will not become overwhelmed trying to do it all at once. Each stage/level can be explored on its own in order to allow teachers to focus on specific aspects of their practice at one particular time. In addition the framework realizes that each teacher will have a different level of experience, from novice teachers at the very beginning of their career to the most experienced teachers, and as a result the framework allows teachers to decide where they want to begin their reflections—either at the very basic philosophical stage/level or reflecting on practice and beyond practice or even somewhere in the middle of the framework in principles or theory. As you will see, the framework is comprehensive in coverage and I leave it to individual teachers to decide where they would like to begin their reflections depending on their needs, interests, and experiences. I will first outline and describe each stage or level in the framework, and then in the section that follows discuss how teachers can consider navigating the framework throughout their careers.

Reflective Moment

- What strikes you first about the *Framework for Reflecting on Practice* outlined in Figure 3.1?
- Can you predict what each stage/level is about?

- How do you think the framework is connected—how is each stage/level connected?
- Do you think teachers can begin their reflections at any level or do you think they should begin reflecting on their philosophy of practice and then the next level and so on?
- What do you think the arrows that are visible in this framework signify?

Philosophy

Philosophy, the first stage/level of the framework, can be considered to be a window to the roots of a teacher's practice because having a philosophy of practice means each observable behavior has a reason that guides it even if the teacher does not articulate this reason. The old behavioral way of looking at teaching as a stimulus-response activity no longer has a place within reflections on professional practice. This first stage of reflection within the framework examines the "teacher-as-person" and suggests that professional practice, both inside and outside the classroom, is invariably guided by a teacher's basic philosophy and that this philosophy has been developed since birth. Thus in order to be able to reflect on our basic philosophy we need to obtain self-knowledge and we can access this by exploring, examining, and reflecting on the background from where we have evolved, such as our heritage, ethnicity, religion, socioeconomic background, family, and personal values that have combined to influence who we are as language teachers.

Accessing Philosophy

Because this basic level of reflecting on philosophy is to gain self-knowledge, we must include contemplations and the concept of "contemplative practice" to help us with this level. As I mentioned before, I believe that such contemplative practice can be considered a precursor to conscious or more active evidence-based reflective practice and that these reflections can lead to more self-awareness. It is not usually the case that language teachers either readily contemplate and/or consciously reflect on the concept of "self," or "self-as-teacher," and so they may need some activities that will enable them to articulate their philosophy of teaching (Farrell, 2014). When they are contemplating, teachers can reach a more mindful state by being purposively more attentive to experiences as they happen, and when they are happening (e.g., in that moment). This can also be called metacognitive reflection and in the next chapter I outline some activities that teachers can practice that can lead to conscious awareness of our thoughts, sensations, and judgments as we teach. These activities can cultivate a type of mindfulness behavior that can help teachers reflect while they are teaching (see discussion on reflection-*in*-action in the introduction to this book) as they become more attentive to and aware of their moment-to-moment experiences in the classroom.

After such contemplations we are now ready to access our philosophy of practice because we have become more mindful and through telling our auto-biographical stories that include accounts of who we are and how and why we decided to become teachers. Such storytelling is necessary to get at the person who is the teacher, because as Bullough (1997: 19) maintains, "personal beliefs become explicit," and in being made explicit they can be reflected on for their true meaning and implication so that teachers can make better sense of their backgrounds and their past experiences. At this first stage it may be an idea for teachers to write their reflections (reflective writing) first before sharing them orally or in writing because the act of writing has a built-in reflective mechanism where teachers are forced to stop for a moment and consider what they will write and after they have written they can consider again what is in print on the page. As I have written previously, over time such reflective writing can lead to a clarification of the teachers' understanding of their philosophy, values, ethics, and assumptions that underlie their practice and even beyond practice (Farrell, 2013). When teachers write about their own lives and how they think their past experiences may have shaped the construction and development of their basic philosophy of practice, they will then be able to reflect critically on their practice because they will become more mindful and self-aware of their past. In summary, reflecting on one's philosophy of practice can not only help teachers flesh out what has shaped them as human beings and teachers but can also help them move onto the next level of reflection, reflecting on their principles.

Reflective Moment

- Do you think teachers should bother to look at themselves as human beings first and only after this look at themselves as teachers, or skip looking at themselves and only look at themselves as teachers?
- What is the value (if any) of looking at the "self" outside the "self" as teacher?
- How can telling one's story help a teacher understand the "self"?

Principles

Principles, the second stage/level of the *Framework for Reflecting on Practice*, include reflections on teachers' assumptions, beliefs, and conceptions of teaching and learning. Assumptions generally refer to what we think is true but we do not have proof as these assumptions have not yet been demonstrated; however, we accept them as true for the time being. Assumptions are thus sometimes difficult to articulate for a teacher. Beliefs in contract are somewhat easier to state and there is a general acceptance of a proposition; in other words, it is accepted to be true by the individual who holds it. Conceptions are more of an overall organizing framework for both assumptions and beliefs and they can mediate our response to situations involving both. All three are really part of a single system, and thus difficult to separate because they overlap a lot, and although I treat them separately in the framework, I see them as three points along the same continuum of meaning related to our principles (see Chapter 5). Teachers' practices and their instructional decisions are often formulated and implemented (for the most part subconsciously) on the basis of their underlying assumptions, beliefs, and conceptions because these are the driving force (along with philosophy reflected on at level/stage 1) behind many of their classroom actions.

Accessing Principles

As mentioned above, teachers do not usually consciously or systematically reflect on their assumptions, beliefs, or conceptions related to their practice and so they must be given opportunities to bring all these to the level of awareness. It is important for teachers to articulate their underlying assumptions, beliefs, and conceptions about teaching and learning because eliciting such details can "provide a meaningful basis for discussion and reflection" (Basturkmen, 2012: 291). In terms of being able to access our assumptions, beliefs, and conceptions of teaching and learning, Richards and Lockhart (1994: 6) have pointed out that this "involves posing questions about how and why things are the way they are, what value systems they represent, what alternatives might be available, and what the limitations are of doing things one way as opposed to another." Consequently, teachers must be provided with such opportunities where they can articulate, examine, question, and reflect on these values and then explore how they are (or could be) translated (or not) into actual classroom practices.

One means that teachers have at their disposal when accessing their principles (assumptions, beliefs, and conceptions) is by exploring and examining the various images, metaphors, and maxims of teaching and learning. Over the years, teachers have accumulated various images about teaching and learning especially during their early school years (e.g., Lortie, 1975) has pointed out that we have spent 13,000 hours in school as students subconsciously building up various images of teaching and learning) and many teachers are unaware of how these images influence their instructional decisions and actions in their classrooms throughout their careers. One way of exploring these tacitly held images is to have teachers first articulate the various metaphors and maxims they have for teaching and learning and then closely examine their use. The images these metaphors and maxims produce become powerful introspective tools for teachers because they can be used as a lens to gain insight into their principles of practice. Chapter 5 provides different methods for teachers to consciously and systematically reflect on their assumptions, beliefs, and conceptions of teaching and learning.

Reflective Moment

- What are your principles related to teaching and learning a second language?
- What are your assumptions about second language teaching and learning?
- What are your beliefs about second language teaching and learning?
- What are your conceptions about second language teaching and learning?
- Did you find it difficult to answer the three questions above? If yes, why? If not, why not?

Theory

Following on from reflecting on our principles, we are now ready to reflect on our *theory*, the third level/stage of the framework. Theory explores and examines the different choices a teacher makes about particular skills that are taught (or that they think should be taught), or in other words, how to put their theories into practice. Influenced by their reflections on their philosophy, and their principles, teachers can now actively begin to construct their theory of practice. Theory in this stage/level means that teachers consider the type of lessons they want to deliver on a yearly, monthly, or daily basis. All language teachers have theories, both "official" theories we learn in teacher education courses and "unofficial" theories we gain with teaching experience. However not all teachers may be fully aware of these theories, and especially their "unofficial" theories that are sometimes called "theories-in-use." Reflections at this stage/level in the framework includes considering all aspects of a teacher's planning (e.g., forward, central, and backward planning—see below) and the different activities and methods teachers choose (or may want to choose) as they attempt to put theory into practice. As they reflect on their approaches and methods at this level teachers will also reflect on the specific teaching techniques they choose to use (or may want to choose) in their lessons and if these are (or should be) consistent with their approaches and methods they have chosen or will choose. In order to reflect on these they will need to describe specific classroom techniques, activities, and routines that they are using or intend to use when carrying out their lessons.

Accessing Theory

In order to access reflections on *theory* teachers can reflect on all aspects of lesson planning such as setting lesson objectives, implementing and assessing the lesson, as well as consciously reflecting on the functional roles they and their students perform or should perform during the lesson. Reflecting on lesson plans thus provides a systemic record of a teacher's thoughts before and after a lesson. In order to access theory at this stage or level of the framework, teachers are encouraged to reflect on their theoretical orientation to planning from among three main theoretical approaches: *forward planning* (teachers identify the content of the lesson first and then the teaching methods that will be used to teach the content), *central planning* (teachers decide on teaching methods before choosing the content of the lesson), and *backward planning* (teachers decide on their desired lesson outcomes first and then decisions about lesson activities). These three designs are at the heart of the lesson planning process because they influence the direction in which the lesson develops, the content, the methods and activities, and the different roles for the teachers and students.

Another means of accessing our theory is to explore and examine critical incidents. Although critical incidents are situations that actually occur during practice, the next stage/level in the framework, I include them now because they can be used to guide a teacher's theory building. A critical incident is any unplanned or unanticipated event that occurs during a classroom lesson, and is "vividly remembered" (Brookfield, 1990: 84). However, incidents only really become critical when they are subject to this conscious reflection. When we reflect on critical incidents, we can begin to understand the theory behind practice. Critical incidents can be written up as case studies as well, so another means of assessing theory reflections is to explore and examine different case studies of specific events that have occurred in teachers' practices. However, both are slightly different: whereas a critical incident is a retrospective analysis of any unexpected incident, a case study starts with the identification of an issue and then the selection of procedures for reflecting on it. Reflecting on both critical incidents and case studies is important because as Shulman (1992) has pointed out, both provide "teachers with opportunities to analyze situations and make judgments in the messy world of practice, where principles often appear to conflict with one another and no simple solution is possible" (p. xiv). Chapter 6 outlines and discusses all these means of accessing theory in more detail.

Reflective Moment

- What kind of lesson planning do you make use of, or should make use of?
- What do your lesson plans contain or what should lesson plans contain?
- How is a critical incident different from a case study? Can you give an example of each from your own teaching experiences?

Practice

Up to now, the framework has emphasized reflecting on philosophy, principles, and theory, or the "hidden" aspect of teaching. If we think of the whole teaching process as an iceberg, we cannot see the part of the iceberg that is beneath the surface of the water (the "hidden" aspect), which is much larger than the visible part on the top. All we can see is the top of the iceberg, or 10 per cent of the whole iceberg, and in teaching this constitutes our *practice*, the fourth stage/level of reflection in the framework. Thus we are now ready to reflect on the more visible behaviors of what we do as teachers, our *practice*, and what actually happens in the classroom. Reflecting on practice begins with an examination of our observable actions while we are teaching as well as our students' reactions (or non-reactions) during our lessons. Of course such reflections are directly related to and influenced by our reflections of our *theory* at the previous level (e.g., see critical incidents in the previous chapter) and our principles and philosophy.

At this stage/level in the framework, teachers can reflect while they are teaching a lesson (reflection-*in*-action), after they teach a lesson (reflection-*on*-action) or before they teach a lesson (reflection-*for*-action). When teachers engage in reflection-in-action they attempt to consciously stand back while they are teaching as they monitor and adjust to various circumstances that are happening within the lesson. This includes reflecting how the students are responding or not responding, how long each activity may be taking and/or how individual students are interacting with the content of the lesson. When teachers engage in reflection-on-action they are examining what happened in a lesson after the event has taken place and this is a more delayed type of reflection than the former. When teachers engage in reflection-for-action they are attempting to reflect before anything has taken place and anticipate what may happen and try to account for this before they conduct the lesson. Ideally the results from the first two types of reflection (reflection-*in*-action and reflection-*on*-action) can be used as a basis for future planning (reflection-*for*-action) and as such are slightly different than the type of planning that was discussed in the previous stage/level of the framework.

Accessing Practice

Teachers have several different methods of accessing their reflections of *practice*. For example, teachers can engage in classroom observations (self-monitoring, peer critical friendships, or group observations), and they can record (audio and/or video) their lessons and later transcribe the recordings for more accurate recount of what occurred. In addition, teachers can use concept maps as a reflective tool to provide insight into not only what may have occurred during a lesson but also as an indication of what the students have learned (or not learned) during a lesson. Teachers can also conduct action research projects on various aspects of their practice in order to gain a deeper understanding of the complexity of their practice. Engaging in classroom observations (self/peer) can help teachers become more aware of their decision making that guides many of their classroom actions and interactions. Teachers can also record their classes (audio and/or video) and later transcribe these recordings so that they can reflect on their practice in a delayed manner. Teachers can self-reflect or can reflect with the help of peers as in peer observation, team-teaching, peer coaching, and lesson study.

Teachers can also consider conducting action research on specific aspects of their practice if they think they need to improve some aspect of their teaching or their students' learning. As Wallace (1991: 56–7) has noted, action research is an extension of the normal reflective practice and it has a "specific and immediate outcome which can be directly related to practice in the teacher's own context." In other words, action research is classroom-specific and involves entering a cycle of planning, acting, observing and reflecting on an issue or problem within practice in order to improve such practice. Thus the findings of the action research are carefully analyzed and some kind of follow-up action is implemented and monitored (which usually involves entering a new cycle of refection). Chapter 7 outlines how teachers can access reflections on practice in more detail.

Reflective Moment

- Richards and Lockhart (1994: 3) have suggested that "teachers are often unaware of what they do when they teach." Do you agree or disagree? Why or why not?
- Are you aware of what happens in your classes and lessons? If you are not aware, what is the best way for teachers to become more aware? If you are aware, how do you achieve this level of awareness?

Beyond Practice

The final stage/level of the framework entails teachers reflecting *beyond practice*. This fifth stage/level of the framework takes on a sociocultural dimension to teaching and learning, which Johnson (2009: 2) points out, is "not simply a matter of enculturation or even appropriation of existing sociocultural resources and practices, but the reconstruction and transformation of those resources and practices in ways that are responsive to both individual and local needs." This is called *critical reflection* and entails exploring and examining the moral, political, and social issues that impact a teacher's practice both inside and outside the classroom. Critical reflection moves the teacher *beyond practice* and links practice more closely to the broader socio-political, as well as affective/moral issues that impact practice. Such a critical focus on reflections also includes teachers examining the moral aspect of practice and the moral values and judgments that impact practice. Reflecting *beyond practice* emerges "out of a dialogic transformative process of reconsidering and reorganizing lived experiences through the theoretical constructs and discourses that are publicly recognized and valued within their professional discourse community" (Johnson, 2009: 98). Critical reflection thus enables teachers to better understand the way our *foundational theories* (philosophy, principles, theory) and our *practice* may be socially relevant or restrictive. Once we become more aware of the hidden foundational theories and policies that we may have unwittingly absorbed into our practice, we are then freed to make our own choices and on our own terms. Consequently, we can begin to contribute to social change for the betterment of our students, our colleagues, our community, and society at large.

Assessing Beyond Practice

As noted above, teaching is heavily influenced by social forces and political trends, as there is the possibility of the presence of different types of discrimination inherent in different educational systems. In other words, no practice is without theory or ideology; every practice promotes some sort of ideology and it is always best to be aware of this. Reflections at this level can assist teachers in becoming more aware of the many political agendas and economic interests that can (and do) shape how we define language teaching and learning. They can become more aware of the impact of their lessons on society and the impact of society on their practice by consciously engaging in critical pedagogy or critical action research. Elliott (1991: 69) defines such critical action research as a type of research that encompasses society as a whole with a view to "improving the quality of action" in that society.

One of the criticisms of reflective practice is that it has been too individualistic in its focus although teachers seldom work alone in a school or institution. In fact, most teachers must collaborate with other teachers in one way or another for many aspects of their teaching lives such as coordinating, consulting, cooperating, and/or communicating with each other even to carry out the simplest of acts in a school or institution. We are engaged in some form of dialogue with other teachers all the time and so we can move this one step further and try to engage in critical dialogue with them as well. Such critical dialogue about practice with other teachers is important and even necessary because as Crow and Smith (2005: 493) point out, "the process of engaging in a critical dialogue about one's practice is important not only in opening up one's reflections to public scrutiny but also, we would argue, in providing an ideal forum for collaborative learning." Such critical dialogue can be assessed by teachers talking in teacher reflection groups. Chapter 8 covers reflection beyond the classroom in more detail.

Reflective Moment

- Do you think it is important for teachers to reflect beyond practice? Why or why not?
- What is your definition of critical reflection?

- How "critical" do you think language teachers should become?
- What is your understanding of sociocultural theory?
- What is your understanding of the moral aspect of teaching?
- Do you think it is important for teachers to engage in critical dialogue about their practice with other teachers? Why or why not?

Using the Framework

The *Framework for Reflecting on Practice* should be considered to be descriptive rather than prescriptive and its main purpose is to encourage reflection at all stages/levels so that teachers can gain an understanding of the relationships among and between the five levels. Teachers can begin by reflecting on their philosophy, or they can begin their reflections with beyond practice, and then reflect on practice, theory, principles, and philosophy, or they can begin their reflections at any point in the framework depending on what they are interested in reflecting on. The important aspect of reflection that the framework is designed to transmit is the idea of change (not necessarily behavioral change but also change in the level of awareness) as a result of going through the different stages or levels of the framework. As Wallace (1991: 54) has noted: "Development implies change, and fruitful change is extremely difficult without reflection." Within the fields of education and second language education top-down approaches to professional development suggest that teachers should change their practice and take up a particular innovation or teaching method that is usually highlighted in a workshop given by an "expert." The idea is that teachers will improve their practice by implementing whatever is being delivered (e.g., a new way to teach writing, reading, speaking, or listening) by that "expert." What usually happens in reality is that many teachers, although they may think the new idea is good, revert back to what they have always been doing because the "new idea" may be difficult to implement. One reason for this is that teachers cannot change what they are not aware of in the first place. In other words, teachers cannot implement any new idea if they are not aware of what they do now. Thus, the *Framework for Reflecting on Practice* presented in this chapter offers teachers a way of knowing what they do so that they can decide if they want to change anything. Along with reflecting at the different stages/levels, this framework provides different activities at each level so that teachers can engage in descriptive, conceptual, and critical levels of reflection (see Chapter 2). When reflecting with each of these activities within a particular level, teachers can become more aware of the aspect of their practice that they are focusing on and then consider the consequences of their findings at that particular stage/level and whether they think they should change anything. When they have finished reflecting at one particular stage/level of the framework they can then move on to the next stage/level and so on until they have completed reflecting within and throughout the framework.

Thus as they work their way through the various stages they can accumulate lots of information about themselves as human beings and as teachers that includes their *philosophy, principles, theory*, and *practices* as well as their reflections *beyond practice*. I will return to the navigation of the framework in more detail in Chapter 9 after readers have had a chance to go through all of the five stages/levels of the framework that are outlined in detail the next five chapters (Chapters 3–7).

Reflective Moment

- At which stage/level of the framework would you like to begin your reflections and why?
- Do you see yourself moving through different levels of reflection? If yes, how do you think you would like to move through the different levels of reflection outlined in the framework: theory into practice or practice into theory or some other movement?
- If you do not see yourself moving through the different levels, would you just prefer to dip into a particular level at a given time and interest in your career as a teacher?
- Do you think anything is missing from the framework? If yes, what?

Conclusion

This chapter presented the *Framework for Reflecting on Practice* for second language teachers which has five stages or levels of reflection: *philosophy of practice, principles of practice, theory of practice, practice*, and *beyond practice*. This overall framework is designed so that language teachers can bring to the level of awareness that which usually remains hidden, the interconnectedness of their philosophy, principles, theories, and practice and also their reflections beyond practice. The whole idea about reflective practice is that through reflection teachers will be able to provide optimum opportunities for their students to learn. The reason they are able to provide better optimum opportunities for their students to learn is that they have become more aware of who they are, what they do, how they do it, why they do it, the results and impact of what they do not only inside the classroom but also outside in the community and society at large. The five chapters that follow this chapter outline and discuss details about each of the five stages/levels covered in this framework.

Chapter Reflections

- The *Framework for Reflecting on Practice* presented in this chapter can be applied in many different ways with teachers reflecting alone, as in self-monitoring, or with a critical friend or with a teacher reflection group. Which way would be best for you and why?

- Before reading the chapters that follow which explain all the different levels in much more detail, which level of reflection would be most difficult or challenging for you and why? How do you think you could overcome these difficulties at this stage of your reflections?

4

PHILOSOPHY

Introduction

In Chapter 3 I suggested that reflecting on our philosophy means that we should explore our "teacher-as-person" perspective so that we can gain more self-knowledge. In order to gain more self-knowledge I combined the concepts of contemplation, where teachers can reflect on the self (more as a prerequisite to more systematic reflections on practice), and reflection, where teachers engage in more systematic reflections on practice. Thus through contemplation and reflection teachers can gain self-knowledge as they explore any and all influences from the past that have been significant in developing their perspectives as teachers. Gaining self-knowledge (much overlooked in the literature on reflective practice, which has taken more of a technical stance (teacher as technician) in many fields) is important for teachers because, as Parker Palmer (1998: 3) has noted, "Good teaching requires self-knowledge." Indeed Parker (1998:3) maintained that "Whatever self-knowledge we attain as teachers will serve our students and our scholarship well." This chapter outlines and discusses how teachers can engage in contemplation that includes reflection on the inner self as well as reflection on our background and past experiences that have shaped our philosophy of who we are as teachers.

Contemplation

The general purpose of engaging in reflection for all teachers is to get some kind of awareness of who we are as teachers, what we do, and why we do it. Becoming more aware of who we are as teachers means exploring our own inner worlds through contemplation. Thomas Merton (1959: 17), a Trappist monk, noted the importance of contemplating our inner self:

> Instead of seeing the external world in its bewildering complexity, separateness, and multiplicity; instead of seeing objects as things to be manipulated for pleasure or profit; instead of placing ourselves over against objects in a posture of desire, defiance, suspicion, greed or fear, the inner self sees the world from a deeper and more spiritual viewpoint. In the language of Zen, it (the inner self) sees things without affirmation or denial; that is to say, from a higher vantage point, which is intuitive and concrete and which has no need to manipulate or distort reality by means of slanted concepts and judgments. It simply "sees" what it sees and does not take refuge behind a screen of conceptual prejudices and verbalistic distortions.

In order to "see" and gain self-knowledge, Anthony de Mello (1992: 25) urged people to just observe and not to interfere with whatever may appear. He continued:

> Watch everything inside of you and outside and when there is something happening to you, to see it as if it were happening to someone else, with no comment, no judgment, no attitude, no interference, no attempt to change, only to understand.

For teachers, hooks (1994: 13) has noted that contemplation is "engaged pedagogy" because it emphasizes well-being: the teacher's and the students'. In order to accomplish this openness and well-being, however, hooks (1994: 15) maintains that "teachers must be actively committed to a process of self-actualization that promotes their own well-being if they are to teach in a manner that empowers students."

So we first try to contemplate our inner world by reaching a calm state of mind because that allows us to become more aware of our inner world, which will ultimately help us better understand our outer teaching world. In order to engage in such contemplations as Senge et al. (2004: 13) point out, we must "let go" of our need to control and our preconceptions of who we are, and we must also reach a "a state of 'letting come'" so we can truly understand ourselves. In other words we must let whatever will happen in our contemplations, happen without any interference from anything. We just observe ourselves and allow whatever thoughts appear to enter our state of consciousness.

Reflective Moment

- What is your understanding of Thomas Merton's (1959) quote in terms of awareness of inner self?

- What is your understanding of "letting go," and "letting come" and why do you think it is important when we want to practice contemplation?
- What would be most difficult for you to "let go" and "let come" and why?

Mindfulness

When we engage in contemplation, we become more mindful because we reach a state of non-judgmental quality of the mind which involves not anticipating the future or reflecting back on the past; it just *is* (Association for Mindfulness in Education, 2008). Contemplation can help us reach this state of *mindfulness* where we can experience an enhanced awareness of our thoughts, feelings, emotions, and perceptions. It is important for us to become aware of our perceptual experiences as detached observers so we can also begin to examine them in light of our conscious experiences as teachers. As Palmer (1998: 11) again notes: "The connections made by good teachers are held not in their methods but in their hearts—meaning heart in its ancient sense, as the place where intellect and emotion and spirit and will converge in the human self."

Indeed reaching such a state of mindfulness can also have positive physical and mental health benefits for teachers and for students (Kabat-Zinn et al., 1985). For example, Kabat-Zinn et al. (1985) noted that after a 10-week course in mindfulness meditation (see below for details on meditation) for stress reduction, most participants reported large reductions in anxiety and depression levels. Brown (1998) discovered that when teachers contemplate while teaching they not only became more mindful of their own attitudes towards their classroom practices but also became more mindful of their students' emotions and experiences. As a result, the teachers' attitudes towards their students changed.

Such mindfulness practice involves participants meditating as Vaughan (1979: 34) suggests, by "quieting the mind, learning to focus attention, cultivating a receptive, nonjudgmental attitude."

Miller (1994) describes several meditative techniques that can be used to "quieten the mind" and help us learn to listen to ourselves, four of which are: *insight meditation, mantra, visualization*, and *movement meditation*, and these can be practiced alone or in combination as they are all very much connected:

- *Insight meditation* (or *vipassanā* which means to "see" things as they really are) allows us to focus on what happens in each moment as it happens. We can accomplish this by just focusing on our breathing: when we breathe in and out we just concentrate on this act and nothing else. Then as we focus on our breathing we can gain insight into the "self" as we watch various thoughts and emotions come and go because we do not react to any of them. Eventually these thoughts and emotions get weaker and finally disappear. In this way we are practicing *insight meditation*. As Hanh Thich Nhat, a Vietnamese Zen Master (2006: 2) states: "To recognize the presence of a thought or feeling is very important. That is the basic practice of a practitioner of meditation. You do not try to suppress the feelings and the thoughts. You allow your feelings and your thoughts to manifest. But you have to be there in order to recognize their presence. In so doing, you are cultivating your freedom."

- *Mantra* means "word" and the meditative activity is to use a "word" repeatedly (out loud or internally) either while sitting or in motion as we continue with our normal daily activities. This type of meditation even pre-dates Buddhism as ancient cultures believed in the chanting power of words as a way of controlling the external world. Buddhism has since incorporated chanting of words that signify universal love and kindness (Thepyanmongkol, 2012). Some mantras (in translation from Thepyanmongkol, 2012) include: "May all beings be happy"; "May all beings be without vengeance"; "May all beings be without ill will"; "May all beings be without frustration." Singing out loud could also be a form of *mantra* meditation as the act of singing can lead to an inner calmness and also be a way of relaxing the mind (and even the body before teaching a class).

- *Visualization* is a meditative technique where you visualize a place (new or old) or a task and remain in a general state of openness while using this place as a type of sanctuary where you feel safe because this sanctuary is unique to you. As you see yourself inside this sanctuary, you become calm and just sit there and totally relax. Because this sanctuary is unique to you, it reflects who you are as a person as you "see" yourself relax and then you begin to notice your personal visualization. Your personal visualization can, as Hart (1994) has pointed out, result in some unexpected imagery and insight because the metaphorical aspects of the contemplative mind are being tapped into. We gain knowledge of the self as a result of meditating on our visualizations because these too are unique to the person who is meditating.

- *Movement* meditation includes any body movement as meditation. The most popular types of movement meditation include yoga and its many different forms, and tai-chi, but even a simple routine such as walking or jogging can also be considered movement meditation. Yoga as movement meditation is very beneficial because as Hyde (2013: 115) observes, it teaches "specific self-reflective skills including compassionate self-awareness and acceptance, staying openness (being unfinished), flexibility (in mind and body), and how to find rest in uncomfortable situations." During any type of movement meditation the mind is focused on "mindful awareness" of that particular discipline, be it yoga, tai-chi or walking. Jerry Gebhard (1999: 215) a language teacher educator, also noted that as a result of his continued practice of yoga, he became "more sensitive to the affective states" of his students when he was teaching. My own preference for movement meditation is my practice of the discipline of Taekwondo, a Korean martial art. For me, the calming nature of the pre-stretching routine along with the practice of kicking and other body movement and postures allows for enhanced awareness of self through attention to mind, body, and spirit while in action.

Apart from the physical benefits of feeling "high" after intense movement (the effect of increased endorphins in the brain), I also have noticed that any negative pre-practice thoughts and energy have been fully transformed into positive thoughts and energy as I go through the movements. Teachers can do simple stretching exercises or whatever body movements that relax body and mind before they enter a class, or they can take a walk/jog during lunch hour and experience meditation through movement.

Reflective Moment

- Have you ever sat in silent contemplation?
- If yes, what was your experience?
- If you have not, try now for the next five uninterrupted minutes to sit in silent contemplation just "watching your thoughts." Was this an easy exercise or a difficult one to complete? Explain what happened as you just sat.
- Read the following statements from the Vietnamese Zen Master, Thich Nhat Hanh (2006: 1/2):
  1. "When you recognize a thought, you may like to smile to it and ask the question, on what ground has this thought been produced? You don't have to work hard. You just smile to your thought, and you now recognize that the thought has arisen from the territory of wrong perception, fear, anger, or jealousy."
  2. "When you produce a negative thought that has arisen from your fear, anger, or pessimism . . . do not suppress this negative thought, but be aware. 'This is a negative thought. I allow it to be recognized.' When you are able to recognize that thought you reach a degree of freedom because you are no longer a victim of that thought."
     - What is your understanding of the two quotes above?
     - What are your experiences with each quote, if any?
- Sing your favorite song out loud 10 minutes before entering your next class. After you sing the song, note any physical or mental changes before and after singing.
- Have you ever practiced yoga?
- If you have not practiced yoga, what movement activities would suit you so that you could practice some form of meditation as well? Try some movement activities before you enter your next class and note any physical and mental changes before and after your movements.
- Which of the meditative strategies and processes above to promote contemplative practice appeal to you and why?
- What other strategies and processes can people practice to achieve greater awareness of their inner self?
- Hart (2004) devised an exercise called *Not Doing*, which he suggests is best practiced when our students' attention is scattered. At the beginning of a class

or at a transition time I might turn the lights off and ask students to do the following:

> Take a few deep, slow, clearing breaths. Let your body release and relax; let any parts of you that need to wiggle or stretch do so. Now feel the gentle pull of gravity and allow the chair you're sitting on, and the floor beneath you, to support you without any effort on your part. Just let go and allow yourself to be silent and not do for a few minutes. You may want to focus only on your breathing, allowing it to flow in and out without effort. If you find yourself thinking, distracted, working on a problem, don't fight it, don't get stuck in it. Just allow it and you to be, and redirect your awareness back to your breath, and to not doing. Perhaps you can imagine those thoughts or concerns floating like bubbles from underwater. When they reach the surface they simply burst and disappear. We might add a ring of a bell, perhaps three rings to begin and one to end, to add to the power of ceremony that helps students to recognize this as special time. The moment of transition from the depth of contemplation to the action of the classroom is significant. As you gently come back to the room you may notice the sensations of peacefulness, a clearer mind, or perhaps a feeling of centeredness. As you move through your day, even and maybe especially when things get difficult, you can take a breath and find that center again.

  o   Did you (students) notice any difference before and after not doing?
- Luft and Ingham (1963) used a technique called the "Johari Window" to help people understand themselves not only from their point of view, but also from the point of view of others. This "window" consists of four different sections that helps a person flesh out different categories of the self as indicated in Figure 4.1.
  o   *Open Self:* The "open self" is known to self and others and consists of anything about you (your name, race, and so on) that is evident to others as well as to yourself; consider that you know lots more about yourself than others do so a lot depends on how much of yourself you may want to reveal to others in order to get some feedback. A lot also depends on how much feedback you receive and are willing to receive from others so that you can better understand yourself.

	Known to Self	*Unknown to Self*
Known to Others	*Open Self*	*Blind Self*
Unknown to Others	*Secret Self*	*Hidden Self*

FIGURE 4.1 Johari Window (Source: Luft and Ingham, 1963)

- o *Secret Self:* The "secret self" known to self, but not to others. For example, some teachers may feel insecure about teaching and even reflecting on their teaching but outwardly they may appear confident to others as teachers. For greater understanding of the self, we will decide what to reveal to others about our insecurities so that we can become more aware of who we really are.
- o *Hidden Self:* The "hidden self" is just that: hidden knowledge that is concealed from others and ourselves and consists of aspects of our selves that if revealed in some manner can produce positive surprises. For example, we may have potential to be good mentors for our colleagues but this potential remains hidden and is waiting to be discovered.
- o *Blind Self:* The "blind self" is known to others, but not to self. For example, we may assume our instructions are always clear yet our students are confused about what they are really being asked to do and so this blind self can be reduced somewhat by asking others for some feedback, for example from students or our peers. When we open our "blind self" we may have the most potential for growth in our level of awareness of who we are as human beings and teachers.
- • Explore each "self" and reflect on how you reveal yourself (to yourself and others) and what you would like to work on in terms of becoming more aware of yourself and your teaching self.
- • Work with a peer or a group of teachers that you know and trust and try to obtain feedback on specific aspects of your life as a teacher that you are curious about from their viewpoint and see what you can learn about yourself as a teacher.

One final point connected to the discussion on mindfulness is what Van Manen (1991) has termed "morally based reflective practice," which he said is characterized by "pedagogical thoughtfulness" and "tactful action." As Van Manen (1991: 139) noted, tact "is the practice of otherness" and "is governed by insight while relying on feeling" so it "cannot be planned." As such Van Manen (1991: 109) has maintained that contrary to Schön's ideas outlined earlier about reflection-in-action where teachers step back from a situation while teaching to solve a problem or consider alternatives through active reflection, teachers "live in the pedagogical moment." This pedagogical moment is embedded in the situation where something "pedagogical" is expected from the teacher—an action. However, the "pedagogical moment" does not permit the teacher to step back from the situation in order to deliberate rationally and morally about the various possibilities and consequences of such an action. However, action is required, even if the action is non-action. That whole active encounter is the pedagogical moment. The reason I included this here is that Van Manen suggests that discussions of the "pedagogical moment" and this type of mindfulness are missing in most theories of reflective practice. I leave it to readers to decide its usefulness.

Reflection

As I pointed out in Chapter 2 contemplation is really the act of meditating on ourselves while at the same time doing something (either sitting or moving) as both ("sitting" and the "sitter") become one; or the distinction between subject and object disappears as we ("sitter") have merged with the object ("sitting"). However, in order to become aware of who we are as teachers and thus get a true idea of our philosophy of practice, we must also reflect on how we got where we are today as teachers and how our past experiences have influenced our decisions.

Because the "teacher-as-person" is at the center of the act of teaching, it matters "who" the teacher is and a teacher's self-understanding is crucial to the scholarship of teaching (Kelchtermans, 2009. As Kelchtermans (2009: 257) notes, "who I am is how I teach," and so the person (teacher) cannot be separated from the craft (teaching). We can capture more information and knowledge about the "who" of the teacher through the lens of autobiographical sketches or a teacher's story. Carter (1993: 9) points out the importance of storytelling because it can reveal a person's theory of being; as he suggests, a story "is a theory of something. What we tell and how we tell it is a revelation of what we believe." Thus stories can provide the best access to a person's knowledge, past experiences, and philosophy of not only his or her life but also his or her teaching life. As Carter (1993: 8) observes, stories, "including those told by teachers, are constructions that give a meaning to events and convey a particular sense of experience." Teacher stories have been called many things in the literature but the most popular is teacher narratives.

Teacher narratives are one of the main reflective strategies that can offer insight into teachers' past experiences. Through telling or writing teachers' narratives, teachers' past experiences, philosophy, beliefs, and values, can be unearthed and then carefully examined and critically reflected on. As Elbaz (1991: 3) has succinctly put it: "Story is the very stuff of teaching, the landscape within which we live as teachers and researchers, and within which the work of teachers can be seen as making sense." Teachers can self-reflect on their philosophy by articulating their stories because these stories reveal the "knowledge, ideas, perspectives, understandings, and experiences that guide their work" (Johnson and Golombek, 2002: 7). Teacher narratives have many benefits, such as helping to increase our understanding of teaching experiences, which can make us more mindful (also see *mindfulness* above) of ourselves as human beings, of our teaching, and of our impact on our students' lives.

The most powerful teacher stories are teacher-generated stories of experiences because these can help unwarp our philosophy of practice (Farrell, 2014; Golombek and Johnson, 2004; Johnson, 2009). By telling their stories teachers can make better sense of seemingly random experiences because they hold the insider knowledge, especially personal intuitive knowledge, expertise, and experience that is based on their accumulated years as language educators. At the same time this mode of reflection offers teachers a safe and relatively non-judgmental environment where they can share any emotional stresses they may have built up over the years and/or the sometimes isolating feeling of being in a classroom (alone except for students) for many years without much reflection (Farrell, 2014). So we tell our story by retrospectively reconstructing our prior experiences and then we can begin to look for commonalities, differences, and patterns so that we can begin to create links between our biographical experiences and our philosophy of practice. I now outline and discuss three ways teachers can approach teacher narratives: *chronological, frames,* and *career critical incidents/phases.*

Chronological

One way teachers can reconstruct their life experiences is to simply tell and/or write in chronological order an in-depth biography that can offer insight into their past to uncover their philosophy of practice. They can do this by mapping out various past experiences and how these may have been impacted by their culture, family upbringing, education, religion, community, and the various experiences that have helped shape them as individuals and as teachers. When teachers have reflected on their story, they can then consider how these past experiences have shaped their philosophy of practice, or if they are novice teachers, how they think it may shape their philosophy of practice. For experienced teachers, such personal story telling can give order and coherence to what may seem like haphazard life experiences because these stories about our past experiences as individuals and as teachers can illustrate the realities, dilemmas, and even the rewards of teaching that may otherwise remain unseen. By reflecting on our chronological story, we can gain some insight into our motivations for what we do, how we do it, why we do it, and above all, who we are as teachers, which is the essential foundation of our philosophy of practice. Pre-service and novice teachers can also be encouraged to examine their personal life stories in terms of the connections between the content of the courses being covered in teacher education courses and their own life history and then consider how these insights might influence their practices when they become teachers.

Reflective Moment

- As mentioned above Kelchtermans (2009: 257) notes, "who I am is how I teach." Is the person you are the same as the teacher you are?
- I have found the following reflective activity very helpful for teachers at all levels of experience when beginning to tell their personal story. I call this activity the "Tree of Life" and it is a good way to help map out our personal history from our very early experiences growing up to where we are today either as a teacher or a teacher in training. The "Tree of Life" is divided into roots, trunk and limbs as follows:

o   *Roots*: The roots of the tree are what you think should be in a tree because they provide the foundations of what has shaped our early years such as our family values, our heritage, ethnicity, religion, and our socioeconomic backgrounds that have shaped us in any way. I will use a real example for each section of the tree: Born Tokyo, Japan to Japanese mother and American (Caucasian) father. Japanese was my L1 until move to US age 4. No Japanese in my US community so had to speak English only. School bullying because I kept my Japanese first name. I consciously rejected Japanese language and culture at this time because of my experiences.

o   *Trunk*: As we move from our early experiences at home we move our storytelling to capturing experiences from early school years all the way up to our high school years and we also focus on any experiences that may have led to developing our perspectives on teaching and teachers, such as a teacher we admired or did not admire. Example (continued): Family trip to Japan at age 10. Partial reincorporation of my Japanese identity.

o   *Limbs*: The "limbs" represent all our experiences beyond high school and include all our most recent experiences and influences. For example, each "limb" can represent an adult experience and/or action that has influenced or shaped our teaching selves. Example (continued): After US university education, returned to Japan to teach English in the JET Program. Reconnect with my Japanese grandparents and as a result adopted a new cultural identity with a positive view of Japan and Japanese, but a negative view of English Education/TESOL. After a few years, studies TESOL got a "real" teaching job in Japan and began to see TESOL teaching as a viable career for the first time.

o   *First outline your Tree of Life and then write up your story.*

Narrative

When teachers tell their personal stories in chronological order with or without the use of the "Tree of Life" as it is outlined above, they rely on their power of memory and sometimes this reliance can be selective and they may unwittingly leave out some important events in their past that have important significance for them as teachers or teachers in training. So some teachers may need more structure when writing their narratives. This structure can be provided in the form of narrative frames which not only provide structure but also guidance on the content of what has to be written in the narrative (Barkhuizen and Wette, 2008). Barkhuizen and Wette (2008) suggest that a narrative frame is really a story template that consists of a set of incomplete sentences that teachers must complete. Such frames, they note, "provide guidance and support in terms of both the structure and content of what is to be written" (Barkhuizen and Wette, 2008: 376). They maintain that this skeletal form will result in a coherent story with all the sentences filled in according to individual teacher's experiences. These stories can then be reflected on later. The only problem with such scaffolding of telling narratives is that it tends to de-personalize teachers' stories because these may not be compatible with the way an individual teacher would like it to be so it is important to keep the frame as open as possible. I provide some different frames in the reflective moment below with this in mind.

Reflective Moment

- Here are some frames you can use to help you generate your story:

Teacher

- o I became a teacher because . . .
- o To me the word "teacher" means . . .
- o When I first started to teach I . . .
- o The place where I teach now is . . .
- o My students are . . .
- o I enjoy going into school each morning because . . .
- o I find teaching exciting and challenging because . . .
- o I do not think teaching is a job because . . .
- o I think teaching is a profession because . . .
- o The best aspect of my life as a teacher is . . .
- o The worst aspect of my life as a teacher is . . .
- o I spend much time thinking about new ideas for teaching my classes such as . . .
- o Making changes to my teaching practice is something that . . .
- o I discuss teaching with my colleagues to . . .
- o What I really enjoy doing in my classroom is . . .
- o I think my students believe that . . .
- o As their teacher I have the responsibility to ensure that . . .
- o Sometimes this can be a little frustrating because . . .
- o However, . . .
- o My legacy as a teacher will be . . .

Teaching

- o Some aspects of my teaching situation that I find very challenging are . . .
- o I'm not sure what to do about this. But one possibility might be for me to . . .
- o It would also be good to get help from . . .

o I had a problem in my teaching once when I was trying to . . .

o The main reason for this problem was that . . .

o I tried to solve the problem by . . .

o It would have been very helpful if . . .

o In relation to this difficulty, the type of research I'd like to do would . . .

o The aim of the research would be to . . .

o A major constraint, though, might be that . . .

Career Critical Incidents/Phases

While narrative frames can provide some kind of scaffolding for teachers when telling their personal stories, they are still open to a teacher's ability to be able to recall many events that have occurred in their personal and teaching lives. However, while trying to recall everything some teachers may miss, or not be able to remember, some specific career critical incidents, critical phases, or critical people that have had an important impact on their development as teachers and on their philosophy of practice. When telling their stories (either *chronologically* or in *frames* as outlined above) teachers can also choose to focus on specific career critical incidents, persons, and or phases as exploratory tools for analyzing the impact of these specific incidents on their careers.

All teachers have a story to tell about something significant that may have shaped us as teachers in our training, early in our careers, or some other time during our career . . . and so do I. In Chapter 1 I told my story from my first year of teaching, which impacted my teaching for many years and still has significance for me. However, I did not fully understand its significance until I articulated it. After that I also realized that I should teach the students rather than the content of the material or consider my students' needs first. So my first teaching story was probably emotionally driven, but it also served to bring some meaning to my initial teaching experiences (Barkhuizen and Wette, 2008; Farrell, 2014; Golombek and Johnson, 2004; Johnson, 2009; Johnson and Golombek, 2002). I shall return to stories and their analysis when I talk about classroom critical incidents in Chapter 6 and again in Chapter 7 and especially how to analyze such classroom critical incidents. In this chapter I want to emphasize the telling of our story without too much structure imposition so a teacher can try to "see" patterns developing in their own stories.

Reflective Moment

• Tell/write about any particular career incident, critical phase during your career or any important person that has had an impact on you as a person and/or teacher. After you have relayed your story try to identify what you have learned about yourself as a teacher, your philosophy of practice, and what impact this knowledge may have on your future teaching.

- Some teachers have had times in their professional practice when things have not gone well. Have you ever experienced any phase in your career that you would consider to be a breakdown where you found yourself teaching without any enthusiasm? If so, can you trace this back to any particular career critical incident, person, or phase such as a negative critical person/colleague entering your sphere of practice?

Conclusion

When we contemplate on our inner self we try to attend and do at the same time in order to gain greater self-awareness of our philosophy and also a better understanding of who we are as human beings and teachers. Such contemplative practice means not only "letting go" but also reaching a state of "letting come" so that we allow our thoughts to float about unimpeded in that moment so that we can really begin to see any conceptual prejudices or distortions that may impact our understanding of our philosophy of practice. Even though we stay in the moment in contemplative practice to reach more mindful awareness we can also reflect on other moments that have taken place in our lives in order to experience "contemplative reflective practice." Contemplative reflective practice includes contemplative practice to reach the inner self as well as engaging in conscious reflections on our lived experiences so that we can gain greater insight into our philosophy of practice. Thus by engaging in contemplative reflective practice we can get a more complete knowledge and insight of our professional practices.

Chapter Reflections

- Edge (2011, quoting Kolb, 1984: 209) has pointed out that "our search for integrity" is a "response to the overwhelming pressures to conform . . . to be the object rather than the subject of our own life history." What is your understanding of this from the position of a language teacher?
- Reflect on the story below (from Anthony de Mello, 1992) and answer the questions that follow it.

  A man found an eagle's egg and put it in a nest of a barnyard hen. The eaglet hatched with the brood of chicks and grew up with them. All his life the eagle did what the barnyard chicks did, thinking he was a barnyard chicken. He scratched the earth for worms and insects. He clucked and cackled. And he would thrash his wings and fly a few feet into the air. Years passed and the eagle grew very old. One day he saw a magnificent bird above him in the cloudless sky. It glided in graceful majesty among the powerful wind currents, with scarcely a beat of its strong golden wings. The old eagle looked up in awe. "Who's that?" he asked. "That's the eagle, the king of the birds," said his neighbor. "He belongs to the sky. We belong to the earth—we're chickens." So the eagle lived and died a chicken, for that's what he thought he was.

o How would you react if I said this story applied to you?

o Perhaps if I then explain that you are that Golden Eagle and you are unaware of the heights you can soar to! What would you think now?

o Do you have any other reflections on the story?

• Our teaching philosophy is shaped by our individual experiences and when articulated can serve as a starting point from which to explore and examine all our other professional principles, beliefs, and actions. Try to write a draft of your philosophy of practice that reveals everything you feel and think and do as a second language teacher and where these thoughts, feelings, and actions originated.

o **Please note**: I consider philosophy statements to be a *rough draft* at this early stage of the reflective process. In each chapter from this one I will be encouraging teachers to reflect on aspects of professional practice and these reflections may lead some to rethink what was discovered and reflected on in previous chapters. So I encourage readers to consider updating reflections periodically and at the very least, after each chapter.

5

PRINCIPLES

Introduction

In the previous chapter I talked about contemplation as a means of helping teachers understand their philosophy. When we teach we are influenced by not only *who* we are but also by our *past experiences* because we have deeply ingrained values, thoughts, feelings, and needs, which were formed since birth, all of which are inseparable from who we are and how we teach. Consequently, developing self-awareness through a combination of contemplation and more conscious reflection on personal past experiences gives us a window into our philosophy of practice and is central to reflecting with others that I will expand on in later chapters. As Rogers (1967: 57) has noted: "If I can form a helping relationship to myself—if I can be sensitively aware of and acceptant towards my own feelings—then the likelihood is great that I can form a helping relationship toward another." In this chapter we continue to developing our self-awareness by exploring our *principles* as another essential part of the process of reflecting on practice and the second stage/level of the *Framework for Reflecting on Practice*. Specifically, this chapter examines different ways in which we can explore our assumptions, beliefs, and conceptions of teaching and learning that make up our principles.

Principles

Reflecting on our principles means examining our *assumptions, beliefs, and conceptions* of teaching and learning. All three have been used interchangeably as an indication that they are similar in meaning, but in this chapter I place them at different points on a continuum of slightly different meanings (Woods, 1996). Although *assumptions* have been closely linked with *beliefs*, however, as Woods (1996: 195) has pointed out, they are temporary and we take them "to be true for the time being." Whereas, Woods (1996: 195) suggests that beliefs are more certain (but not much more) and they generally refer to an "acceptance of a proposition" by someone. In contrast, *conceptions* are more general in nature and encompass both assumptions and beliefs (Thompson, 1992). Because our principles are grounded in our *assumptions, beliefs,* and *conceptions* of teaching and learning, I treat all three separately in this chapter so that teachers can become more aware of the importance and influence of each.

Reflective Moment

- What is your understanding of the terms "assumptions," "beliefs," and "conceptions"?
- Are there any differences to the definitions above?
- At this early stage in the chapter try to answer these questions about your principles:
    o What are your assumptions about teaching and learning?
    o What are your beliefs about teaching and learning?
    o What are your conceptions about teaching and learning?
- What difficulties (if any) did you notice as you attempted to answer the questions above?
- If you had difficulties, why do you think you encountered such difficulties?

Assumptions

Assumptions are taken-for-granted beliefs about anything that seem so obvious to us that we do not usually articulate them to ourselves or others (Brookfield, 1995). Brookfield (1995) has distinguished three broad categories of assumptions: *paradigmatic, prescriptive*, and *casual*.

Paradigmatic assumptions are the basic structuring maxims or adages we use to give the world we live in some order into fundamental categories. For example, in my research I discovered that some novice teachers have as a basic structuring axiom or maxim they use when approaching their lessons, called the maxim of planning, and this means they structure their lessons around planning: plan your lessons and always try to follow your plan (Farrell, 2007a). Later in this section we will examine teacher maxims in order to explore some paradigmatic assumptions that we may have about teaching.

Prescriptive assumptions are what we think should be happening, such as how we think language teachers and students should behave, what "good" teaching is, what "good" learning is, and so on. Prescriptive assumptions are an extension of our paradigmatic assumptions because they are really grounded in them. For example, when examining the maxim of planning I outlined above that suggests the teacher always follows the plan, I discovered that the novice teachers were (1) not aware of it and (2) when they adhered to it, they usually did not include any of their students' interests that arose during the lesson if these interests conflicted with the lesson plan in any way. In other words, by following (somewhat blindly) their maxim of planning, they did not consider any lesson improvisation where they could or would respond to their students' interests; they were not flexible to change their plans.

When making *casual* assumptions we do not think too much about them and we make them in order to understand how things work. For example, we may assume that if we show our students that we can make mistakes in class, then this will help them understand that they too can make mistakes without any embarrassment because we have created such a safe learning environment in our classes. However, our casual assumptions may not in fact be the reality for many of our students who still feel embarrassed when making mistakes using the second or foreign language in our classes, not to mention that some of their cultural expectations may not allow them the latitude to accept that the teacher can make a mistake.

Although our assumptions are closely connected to who we are and what we do, we tend to resist becoming explicitly aware of them because we fear what we might discover if we articulate them (Brookfield, 1995). However, it is important for teachers formally to reflect on their (taken-for-granted) assumptions so that we may uncover any that may not hold true for who we are and what we do as teachers. If we blindly follow our taken-for-granted assumptions, we usually end up reaching a general teaching consensus that satisfies institutions or societal expectations rather than being closely linked with our own personal teaching principles. All three assumptions are actually grounded in each other: casual assumptions are grounded in prescriptive assumptions which in turn are grounded in paradigmatic assumptions.

Reflective Moment

- One way teachers can become aware of their assumptions is by talking about teachers (from their school days, or present day colleagues) they admire. Our choices of these "role model teachers" can reveal our own biases, agendas, and assumptions and in many instances we frequently choose as role models teachers whose qualities and abilities we would like to emulate, and people who excel in the kinds of things we wish we could do (Brookfield, 1995). By answering the questions below we can discover parts of our practices that we may want to develop:
  - o What role model teachers do you admire in terms of representing what a teacher should be?

o What characteristics have you observed in these people that, in your opinion, make them so admirable?

o Which of their actions most typifies what it is that you find so admirable about them?

o Which of their abilities or actions would you most like to be able to integrate into your own teaching and why? Or which of their abilities or talents are absent from your teaching now?

Hegemonic Assumptions

In the previous section I outlined three categories of assumptions that we tend to hold, but there is another category of assumptions that can be imposed on us because they are designed by others and these are called *hegemonic assumptions*. Even though these hegemonic assumptions have been designed by others, we think that they are in our best interests (Brookfield, 1995). However, as Brookfield (1995) has noted, ultimately they work against us because they are originally designed by powerful interests to protect the status quo and when they are uncovered, we can see that they may be constraining or even harmful to practicing teachers.

For the most part, teachers conduct their lessons in classrooms (although I also fully recognize the concept of "classroom without walls" and the use of technology to deliver lessons in distance learning situations). If we consider a classroom as a place where people gather together for the purpose of learning, with one having the role of teacher and the other of student we can notice two important pieces of information: learning is supposed to take place (the reason for the classroom) and that one of the participants takes responsibility to ensure that this learning will take place—the teacher. So by its very nature the classroom gives teachers enormous amounts of power and so as reflective practitioners teachers should become aware of the pervasiveness of this power to see if in fact our classrooms are oppressive environments of learning rather than supportive environments where all our students regardless of cultural, ethnic, gender, or religious background have equal learning opportunities. In this way we can reflect on our hegemonic assumptions so that we can begin to move from a position of having power *over* learners to having power *with* learners (Brookfield, 1995).

The main idea of unearthing and challenging our assumptions is not to be negative about all of them (who knows, many of these assumptions may have merit and may still hold true for you after scrutiny), but to question them and look for any limitations they may hold for us as teachers and then to reconsider the value of any we may feel unsure about. By way of example, I will explore two commonly held assumptions in education: "teaching as a calling" and "group work as valued" (adapted from Brookfield, 1995).

Teaching as a calling is a common assumption held by many that consider teaching as something that transcends a job and "normal" work. It may be that teachers themselves consider their teaching as a calling of sorts or a selfless vocation as in its religious meaning with the idea that those who are "called" have a true vocation and are not just working for the paycheck. Individuals become teachers with the idea that they will make a difference in the world because they think they will be able to enable their students to fully maximize their skills and develop their character while interacting in classes. However, as Brookfield (1995) points out, their selfless service to students and their educational institutions can be tested when they are given increased teaching loads and large classes with a huge number of students to deal with not to mention all the other different roles and activities they are asked or "volunteer" (or as one teacher told me that she was "volunteered") to take. Many teachers of course seem to eagerly take on these extra classes, extra students, duties, and roles out of a sense of conscientiousness (or selflessness). However, I also suspect that many teachers deep down also begin to wonder if their sense of calling has become distorted but think that if they complain because they are becoming exhausted they can be seen to be "whining" by the administration (Farrell, forthcoming).

At this stage, Brookfield (1995) maintains that the vocation has become a hegemonic concept because the "calling" that once seemed consensual and embraced by teachers now begins to work against their individual best interests. We can ask then whose interests are being served. Given that a greater workload with larger classes means a saving of money for the administration, we could suggest that the administration benefits most—the students surely are not benefiting from tired teachers, or from overcrowded classrooms. Critically reflective teachers, as Brookfield (1995) maintains, will be able to see these hegemonic assumptions because they will be able to distinguish between justifiable and necessary dedication to their students' learning and a self-destructive "workaholism" that is fostered by their institution's desire to save money.

Group work as valued is also a common assumption many teachers hold. Teachers assume that such group work gives everyone an equal chance to participate because the teacher respects the student voice. However, as I have seen in a university seminar system which promotes such group discussion, this "respect" for the student voice and opinion usually favors the confident, vocal, and articulate students who have mastered how to manipulate the culture of that seminar. What does it do for our shy students who may be shy because of fear of making a mistake in the second language, or may be shy in nature or by home cultural interaction socialization regardless of the language that is spoken in such a group format? These shy students may feel humiliated when called on to speak in such a group format because they feel pressure to say something even though they may have nothing to say. In fact, Brookfield (1995) has said that these shy and possibly self-conscious students may have been stripped of their right to privacy. Indeed in many second language classes, pair and/or group discussion is nearly a rule. Especially since the advent of communicative language teaching (CLT) many second language teachers interpreted this approach as involving lots of group work in class with the assumption that all students like group discussions. So teachers, regardless of who they teach, may need to be aware of the possibility of students feeling oppressed and as such should continually review how each group is set up, who the members are in each group, and if any do not want to participate. Teachers must monitor whose needs they are fulfilling—their own or their students—and if particular students want to remain silent, perhaps teachers may consider intervening rather than standing back and allowing the dominant students to rule the group.

Reflective Moment

- Brookfield (1995) maintains that we are our assumptions. What is your understanding of this?
- Why do you think we resist becoming aware of our assumptions?
- Examine the two assumptions (*teaching as a calling* and *group work as valued*) outlined above and discuss your views of each one.
- Outline some of your taken-for-granted assumptions about teaching and learning a second and/or foreign language. After reflecting on these and questioning their validity, consider whether these assumptions still remain valid for you.

Teacher Maxims

Another way of examining our assumptions about teaching and learning a second and/or foreign language is through the lens of teacher *maxims*. Teacher maxims, or dictums, are personal working principles which tend to reflect teachers' individual philosophies and principles of teaching and learning a second or foreign language (Richards, 1996). Teacher maxims are usually derived from experience and a guide to teachers' instructional decisions and as such can also be considered as rules for best behavior (Farrell, 2007a; Richards, 1996). Similar to what I said above about hunting assumptions the main point to remember as we (re)consider our axioms or maxims is that there are no right or wrong maxims; however, we now recognize that up to now we may have unquestioningly accepted some of them as truth. When we reflect on our teacher maxims we can uncover our unconsciously held assumptions about teaching, and learning this new awareness can be used to help us interpret and evaluate our own teaching as well as the teaching of others.

Reflective Moment

- Richards (1996) has outlined the following teacher maxims that are popular with second language teachers. Examine each in turn and explain what they mean to you and if they apply to your teaching situation or not. Also consider how your colleagues and your students may view each maxim.

o *Maxim of involvement*: Follow the learners' interests to maintain student involvement.

o *Maxim of planning*: Plan your teaching and try to follow your plan.

o *Maxim of order*: Maintain order and discipline throughout the lesson.

o *Maxim of encouragement*: Seek ways to encourage student learning.

o *Maxim of accuracy*: Work for accurate student output.

o *Maxim of efficiency*: Make the most efficient use of classroom time.

o *Maxim of conformity*: Make sure your teaching follows the prescribed method.

o *Maxim of empowerment*: Give the learners control.

• Wilkins (2009) outlines some more specific maxims that he says may have been implied by Richards' (1996) maxims above. Again, examine each in turn and explain what they mean to you and if they apply to your teaching situation or not. Also consider how your colleagues and your students may view each maxim.

o *Maxim of appropriate level*: Students can perform tasks and not feel frustrated.

o *Maxim of addressing schemata*: The bridge to the new material is built.

o *Maxim of flexibility*: Teacher's ability to satisfy needs of all types of learners.

o *Maxim of teamwork*: Students are ready to share knowledge with less skilled learners.

o *Maxim of cooperation*: Teacher-student, student-student, student-teacher, group-work.

o *Maxim of positive attitude*: Class forms positive attitude towards target language and culture.

o *Maxim of learner-centered class*: Teacher is in the class to elicit knowledge and help students to acquire skills.

o *Maxim of varied types of practice*: Practice is directed to formation of a variety of skills, not one.

o *Maxim of validity*: Teacher provides task that does what it is supposed to be doing.

o *Maxim of cultural input*: Cultural information is presented in the class.

o *Maxim of curiosity*: Tasks are designed to elicit and satisfy natural curiosity.

o *Maxim of perfection*: Students want to become better.

o *Maxim of independent learning*: Instructions on independent learning are given.

o *Maxim of individual approach*: Individual merits are taken into consideration.

o *Maxim of motivation*: Tools for forming positive motivation are used.

o *Maxim of control and feedback*: Students' homework is checked and correction is explained.

o *Maxim of fallibility*: Teacher is also a human, and can make mistakes.

o *Maxim of self-esteem*: Students' self-confidence increases as they progress in the language.

- o *Maxim of using technology:* Technology in the classroom is a fun and effective tool to diversify language teaching.
- o *Maxim of reward:* Opportunities to receive rewards are promoted.
- Amy Tsui (1995: 357) explored the personal maxims of two ESL teachers in the same Hong Kong secondary school and discovered two very different approaches to teaching the same subject, the same class, and the same level. Read how each teacher differs and comment on Tsui's explanation.
  - o One teacher, a Chinese female, was a strict disciplinarian and followed a *maxim of order* that was based on her cultural and educational background, which "valued subservience to authority and emphasized observation to protocol."
  - o The other teacher, a native of New Zealand, encouraged a more informal relationship with his students and his classes were very different from those of the first teacher because of his Western cultural background in which Tsui (1995: 359) points out, "more emphasis was placed on the individual, most classrooms had done away with the traditional protocol, and the relationship between students and teachers was much less formal."
- Now write some of your maxims of teaching.

Beliefs

Beliefs that teachers hold (consciously or unconsciously) about teaching and learning reflect individual philosophies and principles of practice and are usually idiosyncratic in nature (Pajares, 1992). Woods (1996: 72) maintains that belief systems have the following characteristics: they are non-consensual (not everybody agrees, and there is an acceptance of alternative beliefs around the same issue). They often include a notion of existence (something exists). They are highly evaluative (states are considered as being good or bad). They contain a high degree of episodic (anecdotal) material. They have differing degrees of strength (strong or weak beliefs). They have unclear boundaries (there can be overlaps with beliefs in other areas). Different factors seem to shape teachers' beliefs, such as teacher education, prior learning and teaching experiences, personality, gender, context, and culture (Nishino, 2012; Perfecto, 2008; Phipps and Borg, 2009). Some studies in second language teaching and learning report a strong relationship between teacher beliefs and classroom practices (e.g., Kuzborska, 2011), while others indicate a more limited correspondence between teachers' stated beliefs and their practices (e.g., Farrell and Lim, 2005).

One problem with examining teachers' beliefs (as well as teacher assumptions and conception) is that they often remain hidden to the teacher and so must be brought to the level of awareness by being articulated in some. Richards and Lockhart (1994: 6) maintain that reflecting on beliefs and practices "involves posing questions about how and why things are the way they are, what value systems they represent, what alternatives might be available, and what the limitations are of doing things one way as opposed to another."When teachers are given a chance to articulate their beliefs about teaching and learning, they soon discover that their beliefs are very complex and difficult to understand (Farrell and Bennis, 2013; Farrell and Ives, forthcoming). Thus after articulating their beliefs, teachers should then examine the sources of such beliefs so that they can have a better understanding of their meaning. For example, one or more of the following sources of beliefs can be considered (adapted from Richards and Lockhart, 1994):

- *Teachers' past experience as students.* For example, if a teacher has learned a second language successfully and comfortably by memorizing vocabulary lists, then there is a good chance that the same teacher will have his or her students memorize vocabulary lists too.
- *Experience of what works best in their classes.* This may be the main source of beliefs about teaching for many second language teachers and as such many practicing teachers may not want to break an established, and perceived successful, routine.
- *Established practice within a school.* These practices can be difficult to change because the school has always used this method or teachers would have to complete a particular unit in a specific time period.
- *Personality factors of teachers.* This can be an important source of beliefs as some teachers really enjoy conducting role-play or group work in their classes while others are more comfortable conducting traditional teacher-fronted lessons.
- *Educationally based or research-based principles.* This can also be a source of teachers' beliefs in that a teacher may draw on his or her understanding of research in second language reading to support the use of predicting style exercises in reading classes.
- *Method-based sources of beliefs.* This suggest that teachers support and implement a particular method in their classes, as for example, when a teacher decides to use total physical response (TPR) to teach beginning second language learners, he or she is following a method of suspending early production of language for the learner.

Senior (2006) has noted that some teachers may vary in the extent they can articulate their beliefs partly because beliefs are forever changing, and even when beliefs have been articulated, they may be an unreliable guide to the reality of their actual classroom actions (Pajares, 1992). As such, when beliefs have been stated, teachers should monitor their classroom practices to see if there is evidence of these beliefs in classroom practices (deductive approach). Alternatively, teachers can look at their teaching first and then examine what beliefs are being manifested through their actual classroom practices (inductive approach). You will be able to compare your stated beliefs (from the Reflective Moment below) more clearly when we get to the chapter on practices (Chapter 7).

Reflective Moment

- It is difficult for any teacher, experienced or novice, to talk about their beliefs about teaching and learning a second language. Although the following "Teacher's Beliefs Inventory" about "Approaches to ESL Instruction" (adapted from Johnson, 1991) is a bit old, it can help you get started on articulating your beliefs. Read all 15 statements and then select the five statements that most closely reflect your beliefs about teaching and learning:
  1. Language can be thought of as a set of grammatical structures which are learned consciously and controlled by the language learner.
  2. As long as ESL/EFL students understand what they are saying, they are actually learning the language.
  3. When ESL/EFL students make oral errors, it helps to correct them and later teach a short lesson explaining why they made that mistake.
  4. As long as ESL/EFL students listen to, practice, and remember the language which native speakers use, they are actually learning the language.
  5. ESL/EFL students generally need to understand the grammatical rules of English in order to become fluent in the language.
  6. When ESL/EFL students make oral errors, it usually helps to provide them with lots of oral practice with the language patterns that seem to cause them difficulty.
  7. Language can be thought of as meaningful communication and is learned subconsciously in non-academic, social situations.
  8. If ESL/EFL students understand some of the basic grammatical rules of the language they can usually create lots of new sentences on their own.
  9. Usually it is more important for ESL/EFL students to focus on what they are trying to say and not how to say it.
  10. If ESL/EFL students practice the language patterns of native speakers, they can make up new sentences based on those language patterns which they have already practiced.
  11. It is important to provide clear, frequent, precise presentations of grammatical structures during English language instruction.
  12. Language can be described as a set of behaviors which are mastered through lots of drill and practice with the language patterns of native speakers.
  13. When ESL/EFL students make oral errors, it is best to ignore them (errors), as long as you can understand what they are trying to say.
  14. ESL/EFL students usually need to master some of the basic listening and speaking skills before they can begin to read and write.
  15. It's not necessary to actually teach ESL/EFL students how to speak English; they usually begin speaking English on their own.
- Now see which of these (if any) you think you fit into or even whether you agree with the following categories of beliefs:
  Skills-based Approach: # 4, 6, 10, 12, 14. Focus on discrete skills of speaking, listening, reading, and writing

Rule-based Approach: # 1, 3, 5, 8, 11. Emphasize the importance of grammatical rules and a conscious understanding of the language system

Function-based Approach: # 2, 7, 9, 13, 15. Focus on interactive communication and cooperative learning and the ability to function in "real" social situations

- Reflect and comment on the core beliefs of a group of 167 teachers (from Richards et al., 2001) who reported on the practices they thought facilitated the learning of the language summarized as nine principles.
  - o *Selectively focus on the form of the language*
  - o *Selectively focus on vocabulary or meaning*
  - o *Enable learners to use the language/be appropriate*
  - o *Address learners' mental processing capabilities*
  - o *Take account of learners' affective involvement*
  - o *Directly address learners' needs or interests*
  - o *Monitor learner progress and provide feedback*
  - o *Facilitate learner responsibility or autonomy*
  - o *Manage the lesson and the group*
- Now try to answer the following questions to help you clarify your beliefs about teaching and learning (adapted from Richards and Lockhart, 1994):
  - o What are my beliefs about teaching and learning?
  - o How do these beliefs influence my teaching?
  - o Where do my beliefs come from (see sources of teacher beliefs above)?
  - o What do my learners believe about learning?
  - o What do my learners believe about my teaching?
  - o How do these beliefs influence their approach to learning?
  - o What is my role as a language teacher (see also question that follows)?
  - o How does this role contribute to my teaching style?
  - o What do my learners perceive as my role as teacher?

Teacher Metaphors

Another way of identifying our beliefs about teaching and learning is to examine our teaching metaphors. A metaphor, defined by Dickmeyer (1989: 151) as "the characterisation of a phenomenon in familiar terms," is often used by people to simplify their experiences. Lakoff and Johnson (1980: 232–3) suggest that a large part of self-understanding (which is the reason we are reflecting on our principles of practice in this chapter) is the "search for appropriate personal metaphors that make sense of our lives . . . The process of self-understanding is the continual development of new life stories for yourself." Metaphors are also used by teachers as indications about what they think about their beliefs of teaching and learning (Pajak, 1986). Teachers' principles of practice are often expressed as metaphors rather than more logical forms of expression and they appear in the natural language teachers use to talk about their everyday practice. As Calderhead (1996: 719) has suggested, "images are a metaphorical and partly visual way" for teachers to abstract their work. Through metaphors teachers can turn abstractions into real images, and then elaborate on them in order to help them become more aware of their teaching beliefs. Reflection and examination of personal teaching metaphors involves reframing the lens through which a teacher perceives a problem or issue and this, according to Schön (1983), is a crucial attribute of reflective practitioners.

Teacher metaphors (and beliefs) are usually established before pre-service teachers enter their teacher education program and so must be brought to the level of awareness for pre-service and novice teachers. In general education studies Korthagen (1993), for example, discovered that a novice teacher used the metaphor of a "lion tamer" as an organizing theme to explain her beliefs about classroom management as she struggled with discipline problems in her classroom. The novice teacher said that she had developed this metaphor before she entered the teacher education program. After being encouraged to elaborate on this abstraction she explained her plight as being "caged in" and as a result having to "use the whip" or risk being "torn to pieces." This novice teacher's use of the lion tamer metaphor provided a frame of reference for a deeper discussion about how its use could limit her problem-solving capacity as a teacher and an entry into the process of reframing the problem so that other possible interpretations could be considered. Thus when teachers are encouraged to articulate their metaphors they can begin to unpack the meaning of the metaphors they hold, and they can begin to understand what they really believe about teaching and learning.

In second language education, according to Cameron and Low (1999: 88), metaphor "has been used to shed light on the ways in which teachers conceptualize what they actually do, or what they might do in order to improve their performance." In early research that reviewed the metaphors that second language teachers use, Block (1992: 44) discovered both "macro" and "micro" metaphors and the two most common of the macro metaphors used by teachers to describe their roles as: teacher as contracted professional who coordinates but does not dominate his or her students' classroom activities, and teacher as a providing parent who encourages his or her students. For learners, Block (1992) identified two further macro metaphors as: learner as respected client and learner as respected child. Block (1992) later discovered the following metaphors used in addition to the two macro metaphors above: teacher as: researcher, God, devoted professional, comrade/friend, and enforcer. Recently one of the most comprehensive literature reviews on the study of metaphor usage in second language teaching was conducted by Oxford et al. (1998) and their typology covers four perspectives of teaching second language: (1) *Social order*: e.g., teacher as manufacturer; teacher as competitor. (2) *Cultural transmission*: e.g., teacher as conduit; teacher as repeater. (3) *Learner-centred growth*: e.g., teacher as facilitator; teacher as nurturer; teacher as lover; teacher as entertainer. (4) *Social reform*: e.g., teacher as acceptor; teacher as learning partner.

If we closely examine the typology above, we can see that one metaphor teachers use to explain their learner-centered belief/principle concerning their practice is the much used teacher as a *facilitator*. This most usually means that teachers feel committed to a vision of themselves as non-directive *facilitators* of their students' learning. Teacher as facilitator means that the teacher is interested in developing students' full potential and so prioritizes students' needs defined by the students. I introduced the term "hegemonic" above when talking about assumptions and now I introduce the idea of the possibility of "hegemonic metaphors" with teacher as facilitator being one of them. When teachers are following a "facilitator" principle they usually put their students in groups (see also groups under assumptions above) and act as a resource person while giving only minimal instructions about what their students should do and achieve through group discussions. In fact, most teachers retreat and take a "fly on the wall" approach to teaching as they let their students work whatever way they want. However, if we examine this process closely most students are still aware of the power differential that exists in most classrooms (the teacher holds all the power) and if teachers say nothing this can be interpreted in different ways by students: either the teacher is withholding approval or is tacitly agreeing with what he or she is hearing. So we must ask again whose needs are we really serving by the use of teacher as facilitator: our own or our students? One way of answering this is to try to see what we do in our classes through our students' eyes. An example of such a mismatch of stated beliefs of teaching and choice of metaphor was observed in novice teachers by Francis (1995). One novice teacher suggested that her approach to teaching and learning was following the metaphor: "teacher as constructivist" (or a student-centered approach to teaching). However when she explained her actual approach it was the opposite of constructivist and actually followed a more teacher-centered approach to teaching and learning when she acted as knowledge transmission agent. She said:

> I see myself as a teacher who is like the current flowing through an electric circuit. Each student causes a resistance and a subsequent withdrawal of energy from the teacher. The source of energy which the teacher relies on eventually runs down and needs to be recharged if the light bulbs are to continue to glow brightly (Francis, 1995: 238).

Reflective Moment

- What metaphor do you use for you as a teacher? Do you need to use more than one? If so, use as many as you like and try to explain the meaning of each usage.
- Examine the teacher metaphors in Table 5.1 that have been the result of three different studies and are ordered in terms of their prevalence for answering the question: "A teacher is____?" and discuss (a) their ranking and (b) if any apply to your teaching situation.

TABLE 5.1 Teacher metaphors. A teacher is—?

Alger (2008)	De Guerrero and Villamil (2000)	Lin et al. (2012)
1. Tool provider	1. Cooperative leader;	1. Nurturer
2. Guide	knowledge provider;	2. Cooperative leader
3. Nurturer	challenger	3. Knowledge provider
4. Molder	2. Nurturer	4. Artist
5. Transmitter	3. Innovator	5. Innovator
6. Engager	4. Tool provider; artist;	6. Tool provider
	repairer; gym instructor	7. Repairer

- Has your use of metaphor changed over time since you became a language teacher? If yes, what differences have you noticed? What experiences have led to the change you noticed? If no changes have occurred in your metaphor usage, what experiences have resulted in this confirmation of your original metaphor usage?
- Although metaphors are usually expressed in a teacher's natural language (orally or in writing) they can sometimes be expressed in a different manner, such as visually in drawing, painting, photographs, or in guided fantasy. Use visual language such as drawing a picture of your ideal classroom and/or of an effective teacher and explain each. Take photos of a classroom situation (it can be your classroom) and explain what they represent to you. *Guided Fantasy*: close your eyes, turn off lights, and breathe until relaxed. In your imagination take a group back to your elementary school (4th grade) and it is time for your class to begin. Next go 10 minutes into class. Look at the desks, walls, and the class atmosphere. Then return to here-and-now and draw pictures of the classroom.

Conceptions

According to Pratt (1992: 204), conceptions can be defined as "specific meanings attached to phenomena which then mediate our response to situations involving those phenomena." Conceptions can thus be seen as an organizing framework through which a teacher understands, interprets, responds to, and interacts with his or her particular teaching environment (Pratt, 1992). As Pratt (1992: 204) observes, "we view the world through the lenses of our conceptions, interpreting and acting in accordance with our understanding of the world." As mentioned earlier our conceptions inform, and are informed by, our assumptions and beliefs as well as our philosophy of practice. However, whereas assumptions and beliefs operate at a less conscious level and may be driven by emotion, it is possible to consciously review a conception and consider its implications (Entwistle et al., 2000).

In general education Kember (1997) created a three level framework considering conceptions of teaching: *teacher-centered/content oriented* and *student-centered/ learning-oriented* as two extremes and between these two extremes an intermediate category, called *student teacher interaction/apprenticeship*. The first two have subcategories: teacher-centered/content oriented subcategories are (1) imparting information; (2) transmitting structured knowledge. The subcategories for student-centered/learning-oriented category are (1) facilitating understanding; (2) conceptual change/intellectual development. Teaching as teacher-centered and content-oriented conception emphasizes learning content from a prepared curriculum that must be remembered, whereas teaching as student-centered and learning-oriented conception means motivating students to think and reflect about what they are learning.

In second language education Freeman and Richards (1993) used a tripartite classification of conceptions with the following categories: *science/research, theory/ philosophy*, and *art/craft*. This tripartite classification was originally adapted from Zahorik (1993: 23), who noted that each type of conception represents "a set of behaviors that are strongly, but not exclusively, associated with that conception." In other words, there will be overlap between the three and they are not totally discrete skills. Thus science/research conceptions of language teaching are guided from research and experimentation in second language education. For example, this conception of teaching looks to research that operationalizes learning principles, and teaching is seen as being influenced by psychological research on human memory and motivation. The second major conception of teaching, focused on theory/values, is based on what ought to work or what is morally right in teaching. For example, if you follow this conception, you take it that teaching approaches are based not so much on what works but on what should work; or, in other words, based on rational thought and systematic reflection rather than experimentation. The third conception, that of art or craft, is based on an individual teacher's skill and personality, not on any particular system or method of teaching, and so is in contrast to the first two conceptions described above. In this conception, teaching depends on the individual teacher, and not the form of teaching. From an art/craft perspective, a good teacher might see a range of options available to him or her after carefully analyzing a classroom situation, and then is able to select the one that is likely to be most effective for teaching within the particular context.

For Zahorik (1993) an ideal teacher will possess an extensive repertoire of skills but it is impossible for all teachers to possess all skills. So all three conceptions may be useful to teachers but how useful will depend on their particular context and their level of teaching knowledge and experience. This was the case for my own reflections on my conceptions of practice. When I started to reflect on my own practice my early conceptions centered on the scientific/research conceptions of second language acquisition (SLA) but I was also attracted to the theory/values-based conception of the communicative language approaches of the 1990s. As I gained more experience as a teacher I began to move more into a more art/craft approach when I conceptualized my practice approach; this to me was a process where my context in general and my classroom in particular were most important in terms of creating an effective learning environment.

Reflective Moment

- What are your conceptions of practice?
- Would you consider your conceptions of practice to be student-centered or teacher-centered or in the middle as outlined by Kember (1997) above?
- Read the original article by Freeman and Richards (1993) and then try this self-assessment of your conceptions based on that article (Table 5.2). Reflect on each of these conceptions of language teaching. Circle the number (1 = low amount; 5 = high) you think best reflects the quantity their language teaching is influenced by the conception.
  - o Do you think you possess all three conceptions?
  - o Do you favor any particular conception?
  - o Do you think you move through each at different occasions? If yes, explain how you do this and why?

TABLE 5.2. Conception of language teaching

Conception	Assessment				
Science/Research	1	2	3	4	5
Theory/Values	1	2	3	4	5
Art/Craft	1	2	3	4	5

Conclusion

This chapter has provided you with opportunities to reflect on your *principles* as part of the overall *Framework for Reflecting on Practice*. Specifically, the chapter encouraged you to reflect on your perspectives of teaching and learning through uncovering your assumptions, beliefs, and conceptions. Although all three principles are sometimes used interchangeably in the literature, I discussed each separately because I consider them to be different points on the same continuum of meaning related to gaining more self-awareness. Together with the knowledge you have gained in the previous chapter, and the knowledge gained from reflecting on your assumptions, beliefs, and conceptions, you are now ready to move on to the next stage in the framework, reflecting on your theory.

Chapter Reflections

- Examine the contents of the reflections from this chapter (assumptions, beliefs, and conceptions) and add them to the contents of your reflections in the previous chapter.
- What more have you learned about yourself as a language teacher as a result of the chapter reflections?
- What have you learned about yourself as a language teacher that you did not realize as a result of the knowledge you gained about yourself in both chapters?

6

THEORY

Introduction

So far teachers have been encouraged to reflect on their philosophy and their principles and in the next stage/level of reflection within the *Framework for Reflecting on Practice* teachers are encouraged to reflect on their theory. All teachers hold theories about their practice; however, not all are consciously aware of these theories, and some may even deny they have any theory at all. As Stern (1983: 27) commented some time ago, "No language teacher—however strenuously he [sic] may deny his interest in theory—can teach a language without a theory of language teaching, even if it is only implicit in value judgements, decisions, and actions, or in the organizational pattern within which he operates." When we reflect on our theory we can become more aware of the different concepts and theoretical principles that underlie our practice. As a result of our reflections we can begin to reframe our theories and look at our educational practice from a new and critical perspective as we restructure our thinking about our practice. For example, if a teacher thinks that his or her theory of teaching a second or foreign language is all about teaching grammar rules and later realizes that this theory came from his or her own experiences as a student learning a foreign language, we can say that this is a subjective theory because it is not based on any empirical testing. Such reflection can thus lead to a process of reframing theory as teachers begin to look at how they treat grammar in their future teaching. In this chapter we will reflect on theory beyond the level of assumptions, beliefs, and conceptions of teaching and learning to include reflecting on teacher planning, critical incidents, and case analysis.

Theory

A theory is something we use to give us understanding and it attempts to answer the basic question "why?" so we can increase our knowledge of our practice as we realign our thoughts about it. Most teachers tacitly hold speculative theories to explain aspects of their practice which seems to work for them although they probably do not have any hard evidence to back up these theories. Theory helps us give some general label to what we do and what we think we experience while we do it. When we reflect on theory we can realize if our initial perspectives and personal feelings hold true and are what we want from our interpretations. Theory, as Brookfield (1995) suggests, can help teachers critically reflect on their practice in the following ways:

- *Theory allows us to "name" our practice.* When we examine our personal theory even if it is a hunch or non-articulated insight and we see someone else's words that confirm this previously tacitly held insight, we can feel affirmed and recognized. In some cases our privately held insight can be further illuminated and developed once it has been given a "name" because now we may have a better understanding of this because we have become more consciously aware of what it is we practice.
- *Theory breaks the circle of familiarity.* Brookfield (1995: 98) maintains that by reading what others have written we can "get the theoretical illumination of practice in a certain moment." He goes on to say: "If I don't get that, do you know what can happen? We as popular educators begin to walk in a circle, without the possibility of going beyond that circle" (Brookfield, 1995: 98). Thus, theory can "free us from falling victim to the traps of relativism and isolationism" (Brookfield, 1995: 98).
- *Theory can also be a substitute for absent colleagues.* Not all teachers have the opportunity to meet with their colleagues in order to discuss practice and as a result are not exposed to contrasting perspectives of their colleagues. Consequently, the only way some teachers can gain alternative viewpoints is to not only examine their practice but also to read what others have written and said as a source of alternative viewpoints. However, if teachers have the opportunity to have discussions with colleagues, theory then locates our practice in more of a social context as teachers discuss and possibly consider reframing their practice (Brookfield, 1995).

Argyris and Schön (1974) have distinguished between two types of theories that practitioners use: "official" theories of the profession (such as what teachers learn in their teacher education courses and by reading books and journals) and "unofficial" theories which are ideas, hunches, concepts, and theories that practitioners draw on and these are called "theories-in-use." Teachers can reflect on their "unofficial theories" or the theories they consider to be behind their teaching practices, and compare these to their "theories-in-use" or what they actually do in class (we will cover "theories-in-use" in Chapter 7) and compare both. Just as in the previous chapter where we attempted to articulate and reflect on our principles of practice (our assumptions, beliefs, and conceptions), now we attempt to further increase our level of awareness by articulating and reflecting on our theory of practice. As Widdowson (1984: 87) has noted, "teachers must be allowed access to theoretical ideas, no matter how fanciful they may seem to be, but accept, too, that they need to develop an understanding of what they mean and the extent of their practical relevance." It is important to consciously reflect on theory through analysis of teacher planning, teacher roles, critical incidents, and cases because different theories of teaching will inevitably lead to different understanding of classroom life (Richards, 1998). For example as Richards (1998) has noted, a didactic theory of teaching suggests the teacher is in control as a transmitter of knowledge, a discovery theory of teaching suggests that the students themselves can discover knowledge with minimum teacher interference, while an interactionist theory of teaching suggests students actively interact with each other and the curriculum content to gain knowledge.

Reflective Moment

- Do you agree or disagree that teachers base all of their professional practices on some aspects of theory, however it may be derived?
- How can reflection on theory help a language teacher?
- There is "nothing as practical as a good theory" (Lewin, 1943: 35). What is your understanding of this axiom?
- Widdowson (1984: 87): "There is no conflict between theory and practice, only between particular theories and particular practices." What is your understanding of this quote?

Teacher Planning

The first aspect of theory involves reflecting on how teachers plan. Teacher planning involves a complex task of thinking about suitable lesson content to teach, how to teach it including what resources and activities to use, and the possible roles of teacher and students during the lesson. All of these will usually be contained in a lesson plan. A lesson plan will usually reflect a teacher's theory about the nature of teaching and learning, his or her understanding of the content of the lesson, the teacher's role in the lesson and that of the learners, and the methodology the teacher plans to use. Three different lesson plan designs that highlight different theoretical underpinnings for language teachers are *forward, central,* and *backward* designs (Ashcraft, 2014). These three designs are at the heart of the lesson planning process because they influence the direction the lesson develops and teachers should be aware of what each involves.

In forward planning, the teacher attempts to identify the content (linguistic or otherwise) of the lesson and then decides on the particular teaching methods as well as activities that will be used to teach the content. The teacher may also plan to include how he or she will assess what has been learned as a result of the lesson. If a teacher takes a forward design option to planning, he or she "theorizes" that following the curriculum, syllabus, and textbook takes precedence over any other aspect of teaching and he or she also recognizes that tests are centrally rather than individually designed. If teachers are required to follow a set curriculum and finish a textbook regardless of their students' learning, they may be "forced" to adapt such a theory although it may not reflect their real theory of teaching (Richards, 2013). As Richards (2013: 29) has noted, forward planning is used "where a mandated curriculum is in place, where teachers have little choice over what and how to teach, where teachers rely mainly on textbooks and commercial materials rather than teacher-designed resources, where class size is large and where tests and assessments are designed centrally rather than by individual teachers."

In central planning the teacher begins by looking at specific teaching methods and activities before choosing the content of the lesson. As Richards (2013: 29) notes, teaching methods and activities are "developed according to the teacher's understanding of the context in which he or she is working as well as on his or her individual skill and expertise in managing the instructional process and in developing teaching materials and forms of assessment." Such a theoretical focus for teacher planning suggests that "learning is not viewed as the mastery of pre-determined content but as constructing new knowledge through participating in specific learning and social contexts and through engaging in particular types of activities and processes" (Richards, 2013: 20).

In the backward planning process the teacher first decides on desired lesson outcomes and what he or she requires students to know at the end of the lesson. After that as Ashcraft (2014) notes, the teacher decides on what type of evidence would be necessary to show that the desired learning has taken place. Ashcraft (2014: 34) continues: "Only then, after elaborating the goals of the lesson and considering assessment evidence, does the teacher turn to making decisions about the learning activities." Such a theoretical focus for teacher planning suggests that teachers are heavily influenced by needs analysis, planning, and materials development. This may also be a result of teachers having to respond to the high degree of accountability built into the curriculum design (Richards, 2013).

Each of the three planning processes differs with respect to when issues related to input, process, and outcomes are emphasized and this in turn has implications for not only how a lesson unfolds but also for the different teacher and student roles within each design. Forward design lesson planning begins with teachers making decisions related to the content of instruction (i.e., teacher-directed) and only then moves to methodology, and is followed by assessment of learning outcomes.

If teachers design their planning on issues related to the syllabus, the theoretical underpinnings of their lessons are probably influenced by some sort of lists (word lists, grammar lists, or more recently corpora analysis—phrases, multiword units and collocations—to determine linguistic input) to be learned. Wiggins and McTighe (2005: 15) provide an example of a typical forward language-centered design lesson plan:

- The teacher chooses a topic for a lesson (e.g., racial prejudice).
- The teacher selects a resource (e.g., *To Kill a Mockingbird*).
- The teacher chooses instructional methods based on the resource and the topic (e.g., a seminar to discuss the book and cooperative groups to analyze stereotypical images in films and on television).
- The teacher chooses essay questions to assess students' understanding of the book.

Within the forward design lesson planning both teachers and students have specific roles to play. Richards (2013) maintains that the teacher is seen as an instructor, model, and explainer as well as playing the role of a transmitter of knowledge and "reinforcer" of correct language use. During such lessons students usually have a role of producing accurate mastery of language forms as well as the application of learned material to new contexts. They must also demonstrate an understanding of language rules.

Central design lesson planning, or activity-based lessons, starts with decisions related to methodology such as teaching techniques and activities, and issues related to learning outcomes are not specified in detail in advance but are only addressed during the lesson. In other words, when planning such lessons, teachers consider the teaching procedures and activities first, and only later turn their attention to the kinds of support their learners will need to successfully accomplish these learning activities. If teachers organize their planning around methodological issues, the theoretical underpinnings of their lessons will be learner-focused. As Graves (2008:152–3) has noted: "The processes of planning, enacting and evaluating are interrelated and dynamic, not sequential. They move back and forth to inform and influence each other." A recent example of such an approach to planning is sometimes called "Dogme" (Meddings and Thornbury, 2009). "Dogme" lessons are constructed in and around conversational interaction between teacher and students and among the students. As a result this approach to planning emphasizes different roles for teachers and students. In centrally designed lessons the teacher is seen as a facilitator of learning, a negotiator of content and process, and an encourager of learner self-expression and autonomy. Student roles in this approach include negotiator of learning content and modes of learning. Students must also develop their learning strategies and accept responsibility for learning and learner autonomy.

Backward design lesson planning, sometimes called a needs-based approach, first specifies learning outcomes, which will be used as a basis for instructional processes and content. This ends–means approach (the specification of ends as a prerequisite to devising the means to reach them; Richards, 2013) emphasizes learning targets for students and generally has the following steps:

- *Step 1*: Diagnosis of needs
- *Step 2*: Formulation of objectives
- *Step 3*: Selection of content
- *Step 4*: Organization of content
- *Step 5*: Selection of learning experiences
- *Step 6*: Organization of learning experiences
- *Step 7*: Determination of what to evaluate and of the ways of doing it (Taba, 1962: 12, cited in Richards, 2013).

Teacher planning in backward design lessons starts with decisions related to what students will learn (it is pre-determined) and so no particular instructional theory is implied to achieve these ends; teachers try whatever strategy they think can achieve the desired goals of the lesson. As such, teaching methods cannot be decided until the desired goals of the lesson have been identified. These can be identified by conducting a needs analysis such as in task-based teaching or competency-based instruction where learning outcomes are expressed in terms of competencies that must be mastered by the end of the course or more recently the Common European Framework of Reference where particular benchmarks, core skills, performance profiles, and target competencies must be met. As in the other two approaches to teacher lesson planning, teachers and students have different roles to play in backward design lessons. Teachers are seen as organizers of learning experiences, models of target language performance, and planners of learning experiences. Students must learn through practice and habit formation and master situationally appropriate language as well as be aware of correct usage development as they attempt to become fluent.

Reflective Moment

- What kind of teacher planning do you engage in?
- Try to answer the following questions related to planning posed by Crooks (2013: 10): "Think about a course you have taught. Did you start with a textbook, or with some indication of what has been done before, or with a needs analysis? In general, how dependent are you on materials? How obliged are you to use existing materials?"
- Do you follow any of the three planning designs above (forward, central, backward)?

- Ashcraft (2014) outlines the following three examples of each design. Comment on each in terms of their theoretical underpinnings for teacher planning as well as your opinion of the feasibility of each:
  - o A teacher sees that the syllabus calls for teaching language related to the topic of travel. The teacher decides to use pictures to present travel-related vocabulary and have students practice travel-related dialogues from their textbook. The assessment, which is an end-of-semester exam, requires students to match vocabulary words and definitions and to fill in the blanks in a travel-themed paragraph.
  - o A teacher decides to use a group ranking task with students because this would generate a lot of discussion. The ranking task would require students to express opinions using language like "I think" or "In my opinion." It would also require students to use ordinal numbers and comparative structures. Therefore, the teacher determines that the content of this lesson is expressing opinions, using ordinal numbers, and comparing items. After the lesson has been taught, the assessment is created to evaluate the use of these forms and functions.
  - o A teacher identifies (by conducting a needs analysis or by referring to a set of standards adopted by his or her school) that students need to be able to describe a process orally and in writing. This would become the objective for the lesson. Next, the teacher would think of how describing a process could be assessed and may actually write the question prompts and the rubric for the final assessment at this time. Finally, the teacher would determine which classroom activities students could engage in that would prepare them to achieve the objectives and successfully complete the assessment.
- Richards (1996) discovered the following theoretical beliefs that teachers in Hong Kong held about their role in the classroom. Where does each role fit into the three designs above? Which of these roles do you plan for in your lessons?
  - o Provide useful language learning experiences
  - o Provide a model of correct language use
  - o Answer learners' questions
  - o Correct learners' errors
  - o Help students discover effective approaches to learning
  - o Pass on knowledge and skills to their students
  - o Adapt teaching approaches to match students' needs

Critical Incidents

Another way of reflecting on theory is to uncover specific critical incidents and to consider their underlying meaning as an indication of theorizing about practice. A critical incident is any unplanned and unanticipated event that occurs during class, outside class, or during a teacher's career but is "vividly remembered" (Brook-field, 1990: 84). Incidents only really become critical when they are subject to this conscious reflection. When language teachers formally articulate and then analyze these critical incidents, they can uncover new understandings of their practice (Richards and Farrell, 2005). Critical incidents are a very important part of reflective practice because teachers can realize that teaching is complex and that one teacher's experiences may not be too different from those of other teachers. As Brislin et al. (1986: 13) have noted, "Critical incidents summarize common emotional experiences, communication difficulties and challenges to pre-existing knowledge."

Critical incidents can also be general incidents that occur outside the class-room but have an impact on the teacher and can even result in a significant change in the teacher's personal as well as professional life. For example, a teacher might have been so inspired or challenged by participating in a conference or workshop that he or she decides to leave teaching for the moment and return to graduate school in order to learn more about teaching. In fact, these types of career critical incidents can also be represented in the form of an autobiographical sketch, or with the "Tree of Life" as outlined in the previous chapter.

Reporting and Analyzing Critical Incidents

When reflecting on a critical incident teachers can consider the following questions (from Richards and Farrell, 2005):

- Why was this incident significant to you?
- What happened directly before the event?
- What happened directly after the event?
- How did you react at the time of the event?
- What is your interpretation of this event?
- What underlying assumptions about your teaching does this critical incident raise for you?
- Now that you have reflected on this critical incident, would you react any differently if it happened again? Why, or why not?

When reporting such critical incidents teachers can also collaborate with another teacher and share incidents. As Kumaravadivelu (2012: 95) has recently observed: "Teaching is a reflective activity which at once shapes and is shaped by the doing of theorizing which in turn is bolstered by the collaborative process of dialogic inquiry." Such collaboration can be accomplished with a critical friend who can listen and challenge when necessary so that the teacher can hear more than one side of the possible interpretations of the incidents. The "critical incident proto-col" is designed for collaborative work with other teachers. This protocol involves teachers sharing their stories of incidents (see also Chapter 5) with other teachers and receiving and giving each other feedback. The following process (adapted from Brookfield, 1995) can be used by critical friends and/or groups of teachers when reflecting on critical incidents:

- *Write a story of an incident.* Everyone in the group writes a story about a problematic classroom event.
- *What happened?* The story author reads the written account of what happened and puts it into a context of professional goals.
- *Why did it happen?* The group asks clarifying questions.
- *What might it mean?* The group asks questions about the incident using the professional context. Group members act as caring professionals who discuss the case while the presenter listens.
- *What are the implications for practice?* The story author reacts to the discussion and feedback from colleagues and tries to identify new insights for improving teaching practice.
- *Debrief the process.* The group discusses what happened and how the process worked.

Another way of analyzing critical reporting and analyzing critical incidents is by the use of the "critical incident questionnaire" (Brookfield, 1995), which is given to students to get their responses to lessons. It is a one page handout that can be given out at the end of each class, each week, and/or each semester and it comprises five questions as follows: (Brookfield, 1995: 115):

1. At what moment in the class this week did you feel most engaged with what was happening?
2. At what moment in the class this week did you feel most distanced from what was happening?
3. What action did anyone (teacher or student) take in class this week that you found most affirming and helpful?
4. What action did anyone (teacher or student) take in class this week that you found most puzzling or confusing?
5. What surprised you the most about the class this week? (This could be something about your own reactions to what went on, or something that someone did, or anything else that occurs to you.)

Students are asked to give details about what actually happened in class and the teacher can use the results to have class discussions about learning, thus encouraging the students to become reflective learners.

Yet another means of developing insights into critical incidents is by collecting data on lesson breakdowns (Richards and Farrell, 2005). Wajnryb (1992: 87) points out that a lesson breakdown is "a point in a lesson when, due to a communication problem or misunderstanding, the lesson is unable to proceed." The teacher describes the point in the lesson where the breakdown occurred and asks why it happened. The teacher then reflects on how it was or was not resolved. If it was resolved, this too can be documented and discussed. If it was not resolved, then the teacher can suggest ways in which it could have been resolved. The teacher can then determine the personal significance of the critical incident by evaluating the event in terms of his or her underlying theories about language teaching and learning.

Reflective Moment

- When does an incident become critical for a language teacher during class?
- When does an incident become critical for a language teacher outside class (e.g., a career critical incident)?
- Have you ever experienced a critical incident during class? If so, describe the incident and explain why it was critical to you (e.g., what made it critical to you)?
- Have you ever experienced a career critical incident? If so, describe the incident and explain why it was critical to you (e.g., what made it critical to you)?
- What is your understanding of the terms "teaching high" and "teaching low"?
  - o Think back over the past week, month, or semester and consider any incident that made you say to yourself, "This is what makes my life as a teacher so difficult." Where and when did this event happen, who was involved, and what was it that made the event so full of significance for you?
  - o Think back over the past week, month, or semester and consider any incident that made you say to yourself, "This is what teaching is really all about." Where and when did this event happen, who was involved, and what was it that made the event so full of significance for you?
- As mentioned above, language teachers' experiences can be captured through the lens of critical incident analysis and these incidents can occur both inside and outside the classroom. Reflect on some significant change you made in your career as a result of a career critical incident and ask yourself why this is important to you? How will this incident influence your future as a language teacher?

Cases

Another means of exploring theory is to reflect on case studies related to practice. Case studies provide concrete evidence about what teachers actually experience in their practice from their point of view. Reflecting and analyzing cases can show pre-service and novice teachers (and even other experienced teachers) how more experienced teachers have dealt with similar events in their professional lives, and through analysis teachers can uncover their own theory of practice. For example, cases can give detailed accounts of dilemmas of practice that can occur within a lesson, such as a problematic classroom routine or activity, or a learner discipline problem. Cases can also focus on a teaching activity such as a writing activity or a speaking activity or can be more focused on issues of how to set up activities and/or deal with transitions between activities. The main point is when a case is deconstructed through a process of questioning and analyzing, teachers can become more aware of how their theory may have influenced how they acted in a particular situation and if they want to continue to hold the theory or not. As Shulman (1992) has observed, cases provide "teachers with opportunities to analyze situations and make judgments in the messy world of practice, where principles often appear to conflict with one another and no simple solution is possible" (p. xiv).

Reporting and Analyzing Cases

Teachers can write their own cases based on what actually happened in their class-rooms or they can read and discuss cases prepared by other teachers. Olshtain and Kupferberg (1998: 187) maintain that writing and reflecting on their own cases allows teachers "to impose order and coherence on the unpredictable classroom reality where there are always alternative solutions to cope with similar problems." When looking at issues related to cases, teachers can write their own. Here are some topics that can be considered for reflection (from Richards and Farrell, 2005: 128–9):

- Information collected over a period of a semester concerning how two different students (one with high proficiency and one with low proficiency) performed during group activities
- An account of the problems a teacher experienced during her first few months of teaching
- An account of how two teachers implemented a team-teaching strategy and the difficulties they encountered
- An account of observation of one high-achieving student and one low-achieving student over a semester in order to compare their patterns of classroom participation
- A teacher's journal account of all of the classroom management problems she had to deal with in a typical school week
- An account of how a teacher made use of lesson plans over a three week period
- An account of how two teachers resolved a misunderstanding that occurred between them in relation to the goals of a course
- A description of all the changes a student made in a composition she was working on over a three week period, from the drafting stage to the final stage

Teachers can also try to obtain cases written by other teachers to analyze as many teaching situations as possible. Wassermann (1993) suggests that cases (either written by the teacher or someone else) be processed by teachers in terms of three stages:

- *Fact-finding*: Before dealing with the situation or problem of a case, it is useful to generate questions about relevant facts and concepts. During this early stage, the emphasis is on surfacing all of the details that are possible clues for later analysis. This is one way for teachers who jump to premature solutions to slow down their thinking and to focus on the facts of the case only.
- *Meaning-making*: Now that you have completed the first stage of case analysis, you have accumulated a lot of information and need to make sense of it. At this stage of case analysis, teachers attempt to identify the problems within the case from the teacher's view first and then from their own points of view (if you did not write the case).
- *Problem-solving*: In the final stage of case analysis, teachers attempt to make decisions about the case based on the previous set of questions. The last two categories (meaning-making and problem-solving) are for the purposes of promoting teachers' growth in critical reflection.

In addition, the following questions "intended to encourage creative and critical thinking, rather than suggest predetermined views about cases" (Jackson, 1997: 7) can be used to analyze a case:

- Why is this case a dilemma?
- Who are the key players?
- What are the main issues/problems?
- What, if anything, should be done to resolve the situation?
- What are the consequences of each solution?
- What would you do if you were the decision maker?
- What did you learn from the case?

As teachers discuss a case, they define problems, clarify issues, weigh alternatives, and as a result of reflecting on cases, teachers can determine how they may want to restructure their theory of practice and then decide on a particular course of action.

Reflective Moment

- How can teachers who analyze cases link practice to theory?
- List some of the things you think you could gain through writing cases based on aspects of your teaching.
- What do you think some of the difficulties might be in writing cases?
- Suggest examples of topics that would be suitable as the subject for case reports.

• Explore this real case of "The Dyslexic Student" that a teacher experienced and try to uncover the teacher's theory of practice as a result of reading and analyzing the case:

> I looked out over my students on the first night of class and felt a bit of concern. This would be my first time teaching level 4 and the class was large. The number of students fell just short of that required to divide the class. It was going to take longer than usual to get to know these students, and in an eight-week term, that would be bad. In order to really help students, you have to know them as more than just a face. This was a class at an evening school for adult immigrants newly arrived in the US from the former Soviet Union. The students were often loud and self-assertive, but at the same time, many were still in (culture) shock over the changes that had recently taken place in their lives. They knew little of America and were anxious to learn, in both senses of the word. Their aggressive behavior, in fact, was probably a reflection of this. So I settled in with my group of thirty and began. Over the next two weeks, the names and faces began to sort themselves. There was Olya, who was alternately happy or gloomy for unknown reasons; Sergei, who knew everything (or thought he did); Avram, who was both serious and inattentive at the same time; Petr who had already found work as a deliveryman and reveled in discovering different parts of the city. One student I couldn't quite peg, though, was Andrei. He was quiet, not speaking unless required to, but always in class and attentive. He sat next to his wife, Maria, and they would usually work together in pair work. I figured perhaps his being less active was because he had already found work in a factory and was coming to school tired at the end of the day. But one evening, I noticed something odd. During an exercise where students had to read aloud from the book, something I don't usually have them do, Andrei struggled much more than others and more than would be expected from his normal level of fluency. He wasn't the best student in class, but when called on in aural/oral exercises, he was quick to answer and fluent enough for his ability level. So his performance in this exercise was out of character. I decided to check further by scheduling some more reading aloud exercises and they all had the same result. He would struggle along, sounding out words he knew, butchering their pronunciation, where others read much more smoothly. I noticed as well, from his looks, that he really didn't want me to call on him in these exercises. Some further checking back in his school records showed that he entered the school at level 2 and had progressed normally to my level. He was only an average student and his previous teachers confirmed this. They said he was nice, pleasant in class, but a bit plodding. But I felt something more was going on. One thing I had learned at this school was to not let husbands and wives sit next to each other for exams. Too much cheating would happen. In fact I always assigned seats for exams,

putting people I thought might be tempted in the front row. With Andrei, I did wonder if his wife had "helped" him through the previous levels. At the mid-term, I separated him and Maria, but didn't move him to the front because I still wasn't sure (and there were others I was sure of). In the exam, Andrei kept seeming to glance out the windows or was it at the paper of the student diagonally ahead of him on the left? Again, I couldn't quite tell, so I let him go. But after the exam, I held out those two papers and graded them separately. They were identical, and Andrei had a score in the mid-nineties, far above what his earlier records indicated. The cheating I could deal with, I carefully confronted him and made him re-take a new version of the exam. Now he got a score in the high sixties, passing, but barely so! Now I was convinced something was up with his reading skills. I went to our director, a man generally regarded as untrustworthy. He listened seriously and said that the school might be able to supply some help for this student, but that he would have to be tested. After the midterm experience, I knew Andrei didn't want to hear any more about special tests from me. And even if he did agree to this test, I wasn't sure if our director really could deliver help.

Conclusion

This chapter encouraged teachers to reflect on their theory through the lens of teaching planning, critical incident analysis, and case analysis. By examining their planning, through analysis of three forms of lesson planning (forward, central, and backward planning) teachers can get a better understanding of the theory behind their lessons in terms of the focus of the syllabus and lesson, the theory behind their use of methodology and the different roles for teachers and students that are encouraged in such lessons. By detailing, analyzing, and interpreting important critical incidents and case studies, teachers (both experienced and novice teachers) are also provided with further opportunities to reflect on and consolidate their philosophical and theoretical understanding of their practices and if they desire, can even go on to further and more detailed exploration of different aspects of teaching through detailed action research projects. Analyzing critical incidents and cases based on descriptions of how teachers (either self-developed or written by other teachers) deal with issues encountered in the classroom and beyond the classroom can provide a basis for arriving at valuable insights and theories, while also enabling teachers to verbalize and share their theoretical and practical problem-solving strategies they make in their practice. It is important for teachers to reflect on their theory because although it may sound appealing, teachers should nevertheless examine its feasibility so that they may come to further develop their understanding of practice. The previous three chapters reflected on teachers' philosophy (Chapter 4), principles (Chapter 5) and theory (Chapter 6). I believe that these make up teachers' "theoretical foundations of practice." The next chapter encourages teachers to reflect on their practice.

Chapter Reflections

- Write an official platform of your "foundations of practice". This platform will articulate your philosophy (Chapter 4), principles (Chapter 5), and theory (Chapter 6) that guide your professional practice.
- Write a letter to a trusted friend/colleague that summarizes your "foundations of practice" so that your friend/colleague will understand your philosophy, principles, and theory of practice and why this knowledge is important to you as a second language teacher.

7

PRACTICE

Introduction

The previous three chapters reflected on the philosophy, principles, and theory that combine to make up teachers'"theoretical foundations of practice," and this chapter proceeds onto reflecting on practice. Practice is stage/level 4 of the *Framework for Reflecting on Practice*. In this chapter teachers are encouraged to systematically reflect on their practice to see what they actually do in lessons (rather than what they believe they do). As a result of reflecting on practice, teachers can come to develop new understanding and insights about students, teaching, and themselves as teachers and compare the results with the knowledge they have collected from reflecting on their "theoretical foundations of practice." In this manner teachers can examine if and how their theoretical foundations influence practice and if and how practice influences their theoretical foundations. This chapter first discusses how teachers can reflect *in, on,* and *for* action, and then outlines and describes how teachers can reflect on their practice by engaging in classroom observations (self and peer observation). The chapter also covers how teachers can plan action research projects as a result of reflecting on practice.

Reflecting *In, On, For* Action

Previously I mentioned that teachers can reflect-*in-on-for*-action as they explore their classroom practice. Reflection-*in*-action occurs when teachers are in the act of teaching. In order for teachers to be able to reflect-in-action they must, as Schön (1987: 30) has noted, "exhibit a kind of knowing-in-practice, most of which is tacit." Knowing-in-practice is analogous to seeing and recognizing a face in a crowd without "listing" and piecing together separate features. If anyone had to do this, it would be very difficult (try it!). Reflection-in-action begins with teachers experiencing some kind of internal dialogue where they access their thoughts and feelings while they are teaching (Schön, 1987). As Schön (1987: 26) points out, "In the midst of action our thinking serves to reshape what we are doing while we are doing it [and] when we can still make a difference to the situation at hand."

Reflection-*on*-action (Schön 1983, 1987) differs from reflection-in-action as it is more delayed and happens further away from the classroom events. Here teachers reflect on events after the class, such as how instructions were given and understood, the impact of the lesson (what was learned, and what needs to be redone), how classroom communication either provided or blocked opportunities for learning, or many other different aspects of the classroom events that have occurred. Reflection-*on*-action can be undertaken by teachers with any level of experience and as such will be highlighted in this chapter through the broad lens of classroom observation. As a result of reflecting-*on*- action, teachers can consider adjusting their practice for future improvement, or their reflections-*for*- action.

Reflection-*for*-action is different from the previous notions of reflection, then, in that it is proactive in nature and can be the desired outcome of both reflection-in-action and reflection-on-action. Along with combining the knowledge gained from classroom observations during and after class, reflecting for action can also be facilitated through conducting action research projects on the results of the previous modes of reflection.

The main purpose, then, for reflecting on practice regardless of what stage of the *Framework for Reflecting on Practice* teachers begin their reflections, teachers must know exactly what they do before they try to change anything. This may seem obvious but reflection on practice means knowing what we *actually* do in class rather than what we *think* we do. So we can prepare for future action using the knowledge gained from exploring what happened *during* a class and what was reflected on *after* a class so that we can look for any inconsistencies between our foundational theories and our actual classroom teaching practices. We will first explore reflection-*in/on/for*-action through the general lens of observation and then through the reflective tool of action research.

Reflective Moment

- Try to think about your teaching while you teach (you may write down on a piece of paper your thoughts at various times during the lesson if you get a chance).

Classroom Observation

Because classrooms are such busy places, with many different activities happening at the same time, much of what is happening in that classroom remains largely unknown to the teacher (Richards and Lockhart, 2004). However, by system-atically reflecting on classroom teaching and student learning, language teachers can develop greater awareness of not only instructional processes and decision making but also student learning. One of the most common ways of reflecting *on* (*in* and *for*) classroom teaching is to engage in classroom observations. Cogan's (1973: 134) has defined classroom observations as "those operations by which individuals make careful, systematic scrutiny of the events and interactions occurring during classroom instruction. The term also applies to the records made of these events and interactions." Observations can be carried out either alone, with the use of a recorder (audio/video), and/or having a peer or facilitator observe classes.

Reflective Moment

- Philip Jackson (1968: 11) reminds us that a teacher "engages in as many as 1000 interpersonal interchanges each day." How many interpersonal interactions do you engage in each day, each class? If a lesson is such a dynamic event during which many things occur simultaneously, how can teachers hope to become aware of everything that is happening in their classrooms?
- Good and Brophy (1991: 26–7) have outlined the following classroom problems that occurred because of lack of teacher awareness of their own behavior in the classroom:
  o Teacher domination
  o Lack of emphasis on meaning
  o Overuse of factual questions
  o Few attempts to motivate students
  o Not cognizant of effects of seat location and grouping
  o Over-reliance on repetitive seatwork
    ▪ Have you ever experienced any of these problems in your teaching? If yes, explain what happened and how you reacted.
    ▪ Try to think of other problems that could occur in teaching if a teacher is not aware of his or her behavior and actions in the classroom.
- In order for classroom observations to succeed Gebhard (1999: 35) has pointed out that they should entail: "Nonjudgmental description of class-room events that can be analyzed and given interpretation." What is your understanding of nonjudgmental observations?

Process

In order to conduct classroom observations, teachers can explore their own teaching by gathering data from audio and/or video recordings and examine these after the class and/or they can get a colleague to observe the class. The first type is called *self-observation* and the second type is called *peer-observation*.

Self-observation

Self-observation is a systematic approach to "the observation, evaluation, and management of one's own behavior" (Richards, 1990: 118) in order to have a better understanding of teaching and ultimately to gain better control over it. Teachers can observe themselves while they teach as in reflection-*in*-action or they can observe themselves after the class (such as reflection-*on*-action). Richards (1990: 118) defines self-observation as a "teacher making a record of a lesson, either in the form of a written account or an audio or video recording of a lesson, and using the information obtained as a source of feedback on his or her teaching." An example of a written account of a lesson is when a teacher reflects with the use of a self-report either quantitatively or qualitatively. Self-reporting using a quantitative approach involves completing a checklist of some sort in which the teacher marks which practices were used during the lesson and how often they were used. The accuracy of self-reports increases when teachers focus their reflections on the teaching of specific skills and when the self-report is constructed to reflect a wide range of teaching behaviors (Richards, 1990). When teachers use self-reports over a period of time, they can discover the kinds of activities they use or favor, and the kinds of activities that worked well or did not work well.

Tally sheets, although they can be open to misinterpretation, can also be used for self-reflection as they are easy to use to focus on specific elements of teaching. The following example of a tally sheet for describing group interaction was used by a teacher group I was working with in Asia and may be helpful to get teachers started in thinking about and ultimately making their own tally sheet that best meets their particular needs and the needs of their students (Farrell, 2007a). The tally sheet was used to monitor small group interaction within group work where a small number of students were working together and alone; in other words the teacher was not controlling the interaction and task completion in the group. This tally sheet helped the teacher determine how the group used its time when completing a required task. The teacher coded every 10 to 15 seconds to illustrate what the group is doing at that particular moment and then looked at the pattern that emerged over the task completion time.

Task	Frequency
Discussion in target language	_____
Discussion in native language	_____
On-task discussion: general group	_____
On-task discussion: one/two dominate	_____
Off-task discussion	_____
Group silence	_____

This same tally sheet can be adjusted to monitor the involvement and participation of individual students during group work when the teacher chooses one particular student (or observes different students within one group every few minutes) from one group and observes this student every 10 to 15 seconds and makes an entry.

When a teacher "observes" his or her own teaching in a reflection-on-action mode of reflection, he or she can make use of equipment such as a tape recorder and/or a video recorder and then transcribe the contents after the recording. Teachers may want to start first with audio recording their class before video-taping their class, as audio-recording classes may be less threatening (also for their students). When teachers have gotten used to hearing their own voice while teaching and maybe had some practice transcribing what they hear, they can move on to video-taping their classes. Both teachers and students may need more time to get used to having a video camera in their classroom and for this reason, teachers should place a video camera in each class for a period of time (about two weeks) so that all are used to having the camera in the class. Otherwise, the data gathered will be over influenced by the "Ripple Effect"—when we throw a stone in water, it produces ripples; when we have an observer and/or tape recorder/video camera in class, it too changes the normalcy of the lesson. We can never get rid of the "Ripple Effect"; however, we can try and minimize it by giving time to getting used to having the class observed (mechanically or otherwise).

When teachers use audio and video recordings of their classes to learn about their teaching, they have to make some choices about how they will analyze what they see and hear. Audio and videotapes have one advantage over having a classroom observer: they can be listened to many times and videotapes can be watched as often as a teacher desires. Teachers can transcribe all or parts of a tape (both audio and video). If teachers have a direct focus and reason for the classroom observation (such as an examination of the type of questions they ask), they can transcribe the relevant parts only (such as every time the teacher asks a question). However, by transcribing all of the class, a teacher can have a better chance to observe patterns in his or her teaching. This will help the teacher make a general exploration of all aspects of his or her teaching. Later the teacher can focus in and conduct an action research project on some aspect of his or her teaching.

Reflective Moment

- Bring in a tape recorder and tape yourself teaching a number of classes. What is your reaction to hearing yourself talk in the classroom?
- Likewise, bring in a video camera and tape your class. Again, what is your reaction to seeing and hearing yourself teaching? What is your reaction to seeing your students in class?
- Make lists for both audio and video recording about what you learned in terms of your teaching, your students' learning and these methods of obtaining information about your class.
- What topics would you like to focus your classroom observation on? List these topics in order of importance to you. Examples could include:
  - Where do I look when I am teaching my class (use of video: the teacher's action zone)?

- o How do I begin and end my classes (audio and video)?
- o How do I give instructions (audio and video)?
- o How do I give feedback (video and audio)?
- o Try to list more.
- Explore the following topics for focused classroom observations and self-reports:
  - o *Teacher's time management:* Allotment of time to different activities during the lesson.
  - o *Students' performance on tasks:* Their strategies, procedures, and interaction patterns.
  - o *Teacher's action zone:* The extent to which the teacher interacted with some students more frequently than others during a lesson.
  - o *Use of the textbook:* The extent to which a teacher used the textbook during a lesson and the types of departures made from it.
  - o *Pair work:* The way students completed a pair-work task, the responses they made during the task, the type of language they used.
  - o *Group work:* Students' use of L1 versus L2 during group work, students' time-on-task during group work, and the dynamics of group activities.
  - o *Classroom interaction:* The different types of seating arrangements that provide opportunities (or block opportunities) for more student participation and language development.
  - o *Lesson structure:* The nature and impact of the learning activities.
  - o *Classroom communication:* The communication patterns evident, including the teacher's use of questioning, that either promote or block opportunities for learning.
- Review your recorded lesson and try to answer the following questions:
  - o What did I do well?
  - o What did I do not so well?
  - o Did I learn anything unexpected about my teaching?
  - o What kind of teaching characterized the lesson?
  - o Were there ample opportunities for learning and for student participation?
  - o How well did I do in relation to the following aspects of the lesson:
    - o Pacing
    - o Explanations
    - o Questions
    - o Feedback to students
    - o Creating a positive and supportive atmosphere

Peer Observations

In terms of collecting information from classroom observations, it may be difficult for any teacher, and especially a novice teacher, to really "see" and then analyze, interpret, and reflect critically on his or her teaching. Consequently, it may be more helpful if a teacher has the assistance of another "pair of eyes" such as a peer who observes the class in real time. As Cogan (1973: 138) has indicated: "The advantage of an observer over the tape recorder is that the former can be specially trained to record selectively, to shift his attention to a pre-specified speaker when several individuals are speaking at the same time, and to record only certain types of events." When two (or more) teachers work together to observe practice they can help each other "notice" that something may not be in tune between their beliefs and practices (see also the discussion on critical incidents in the previous chapter). Herein is the essence of reflecting on practice: "noticing" something is "off" in practice and a peer or critical friend acting as another set of eyes in the classroom and/or while listening to a recording and/or watching a video together after the class. If improving practice is the purpose of peer reflections, then whatever is "noticed" will probably be a particular teaching skill such as how many, and what kind of questions a teacher asks or indeed how long a teacher waits after asking a question (wait-time).

Such was the case when I recently acted as a critical friend for an experienced ESL teacher in Canada. The teacher had a general perceived purpose for inviting me to observe her teaching as improving her practice. Because both of us were familiar with an observation instrument called a SCORE chart, or a seating chart observation record (Acheson and Gall, 1987), we choose to use this to aid us in our reflections. SCORE is an observation instrument that codes the communication flows in the classroom and is usually used while the lesson is proceeding but it can also be done later with video and/or audio tapes but I would suggest the latter may not be as accurate as so much depends on the quality of the recordings. The advantage of using an observation such as SCORE is that it helps focus the observer on specific classroom actions that require low-inferences by the observer. Coding is based on evidence rather than the observer's opinion. As Day (1990: 51) notes, the SCORE instrument is useful to look at "teacher and student talk; at task; and movement patterns" and the teacher said she was interested in this aspect of her teaching when informed about a SCORE analysis because a SCORE can give a detailed description of the teacher's questioning behaviors such as:

* How many whole class questions does the teacher ask?
* How many students answer these whole class questions?
* How many individual questions does the teacher ask?
* How many students answer these individual questions?
* Who does the teacher ask the most individual questions?
* Where are they sitting? What part of the classroom?
* Which gender does the teacher call on most?

Use of this instrument also focuses the post-observation conference discussion and because it is easy to familiarize the teacher with the SCORE process ahead of time, there will not be too many disagreements about what just happened. Of course, some may say that the above advantages can also be a constraint on the observation process because people will not know what to do if something happens that is not covered by the categories in SCORE. While this is true, for a novice teacher such low-inference observation instruments may be more useful because they can focus separately on different features of classroom interaction, including verbal, paralinguistic, non-linguistic, cognitive, affective, and discourse features (Chaudron, 1988). In this way, novice teachers can become more familiarized with important aspects of teaching in a real context in small doses rather than become submerged with more open-ended, high-inference category systems that do not really contribute to their professional development.

One class in particular stood out, a conversation class, and as an observer I recorded 23 minutes of classroom interaction during that particular class as outlined in Figure 7.1.

The SCORE chart in Figure 7.1 generally indicates that two students (see arrows from teacher to both) M3 (male student) and F2 (female student) were the most active as they answered 65 of the total of 105 questions asked by the teacher (or 65 per cent of the total questions) during that 23 minute period of the class. On the other extreme end of this was the reality that three students (M5, F3, and F4) did not speak at all during the 23 minutes. I gave the teacher the SCORE at the end of the class and she noticed this pattern and commented that in recent classes "M3 always tended to shout out answers before anyone else had a chance to speak" and as she reflected this had been "an ongoing management issue to acknowledge and yet restrain him allowing others opportunity to answer." As a result of our post-observation discussion using the SCORE chart as a reflective tool, the teacher noted that now she "has become more aware of her questioning" and that she would consider this discovery the next time she met that class. When she met the class next (I did not observe) she said that she shared the SCORE

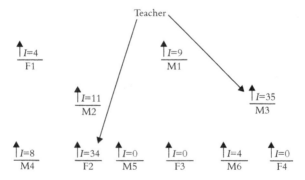

FIGURE 7.1 Strengths, challenges, opportunities, responses, effectiveness (SCORE) analysis

chart and told the class "in a joking way" that she "needed to ask those quiet-types more questions." However, both M3 and F2 continued to shout answers regardless of who the teacher asked but this time the teacher said that she ignored them or she used "body language and eye contact to get the responses of others. I continued to include them but just didn't pay attention when they yelled out." Although she said that she felt somewhat nervous at first with this new questioning and response pattern, she also felt more in control of the class and eventually M3 and F2 were a bit calmer and did not shout out as much. She also noted that the SCORE analysis showed her patterns of classroom interaction that "would have otherwise gone unnoted." She continued: "The SCORE analysis gave me a kind of snapshot of my classroom interaction and as a result I could "see" what patterns were most prevalent." She then noted that it was up to her how she used it and she decided to use it as a "teaching aid to help me better communicate to the students the need for all of them to participate."

The classroom and the use of a SCORE chart as a reflective tool provided the observer (me) and the teacher with a means of discussing in concrete terms (from the SCORE) interactional patterns and their result on language learning in the teacher's particular classroom. When teachers engage in such classroom observations as part of their reflective practice, they can as Day (1990: 43) has noted, "develop a terminology for understanding and discussing the teaching process; develop an awareness of the principles and decision making that underlie effective teaching and distinguish between effective and ineffective classroom practices." When conducted with the aid of a facilitator, peer, and/or critical friend who observes in a nonjudgmental manner such as with the use of a non-inferential observation instrument such as the SCORE chart used in the case outlined above, they can give voice to a teacher's thinking while at the same time being heard in a sympathetic but constructively critical way. In addition, the results of the observation can lead to some interesting action research projects (see next section in this chapter).

Another form of peer observations is team teaching. Team teaching is an undertaking whereby two or more teachers team-up as equals as they take responsibility for planning, teaching and evaluating a class a series of classes or even a whole course (Richards and Farrell, 2005). Such a team-teaching arrangement provides a ready-made classroom observation situation but without any evaluative component and also provides more opportunities for individual student interaction with a teacher because there is more than one teacher in the room (Farrell, 2007a). Team teaching must also allow for teachers who have differing personalities, teaching styles, and even planning styles. In order to accommodate such differences, Struman (1992: 169) suggests that the team consider "The principle of flexible equality" whereby teachers with different personalities acknowledge these differences and do not try to avoid or bury them. Instead, the teachers can define their roles and responsibilities that are most suitable for their own individual needs and situations. Richards and Farrell (2005) outline some of the following team teaching arrangements that teams can choose from depending on what best meets their needs:

- *Equal partners:* Both teachers see themselves as having equal experiences and knowledge and so all decisions are shared equally for all stages of the lesson: planning, delivery, monitoring, and checking.
- *Leader and participant:* One teacher is given or assumes a leadership role because he or she has more experience with team teaching.
- *Mentor and apprentice:* One teacher is recognized as an expert teacher (and thus takes more responsibility) while the other is a novice.
- *Native/Advanced speaker and less proficient speaker:* In some situations (such as in Japan's JET program) a native English language speaker or an advanced speaker of English may team teach with a less proficient speaker. In some cases the native/advanced speaker takes responsibility for those aspects of the lesson that are more linguistically demanding but in many cases the lesson takes place in the less proficient speaker's class so he or she must take responsibility for setting up the lesson.

Linked to team teaching is another form of peer observation called lesson study (see also teacher planning in Chapter 5). Johnson (2009) points out that lesson study is teacher-directed, collaborative, non-evaluative, and grounded in everyday classroom practices. In lesson study Johnson (2009) reports that teams of teachers co-plan a lesson that usually focuses on a particular content or unit of study. After the lesson, the team (the teacher, observers, and any outside experts invited) gather together to discuss their observations. After the group discussions, the team revisits the lesson based on the feedback they received and a revised lesson is then delivered either to the same class or to a different group of students. A second review is held that focuses on the overall effectiveness of the lesson. The lesson study cycle ends with the team publishing a report, which includes lesson plans, observed student behavior, teacher reflections, and a summary of the group discussions.

Also linked to peers helping each other observe and reflect is peer coaching, which focuses specifically on the process of teaching and on how two teachers can collaborate to help one or both teachers improve some aspect of their teaching. Peer coaching has the following characteristics: two teachers decide on a collaborative relationship; the two plan a series of opportunities to explore teaching collaboratively; one adopts the role of coach and they undertake a joint project or activity that involves collaborative learning; the coach provides feedback and suggestions (Richards and Farrell, 2005). Classroom observations can be phased-into peer coaching in a typical developmental classroom observation four-step sequence of pre-observation discussion, actual classroom visit, post-visit discussion, and general review of the process. Peer observations, team teaching, lesson study, and peer-coaching arrangements all combine Robbins's (1991: 1) ideas of teachers reflecting together on current practices in order to "expand, refine, and build new skills, share ideas; teach one another; conduct classroom research; or solve problems in the workplace."

Reflective Moment

* Richards and Lockhart (1994) suggest that a learner's interactional competence in terms of their understanding of the rules of classroom interaction consist of them knowing the classroom etiquette that is required. In addition, Richards and Lockhart (1994) have identified six *interactional styles* that are personified by the following six types of learner:
  o   Task-oriented learners
  o   "Phantom" learners
  o   Social learners
  o   Dependent learners
  o   Isolated learners
  o   Alienated learners
    * Are the students required to raise their hands and wait to be nominated before asking or answering a question, or can they shout out and participate more spontaneously in your classes?
    * What level of formality operates within your class?
    * How and when are students expected to interact with other students?
    * Can students move around the room whenever they want?
    * If a student needs help with something, when and how does the student approach you?
    * To what extent are your students free to challenge what you say?
    * Can you identify any of the six interactional styles in your current students?
* Ask a peer to join you for classroom observations in a team-teaching arrangement, lesson study group and/or peer-coaching arrangement. Decide on what aspects of your teaching you would like to look at and/or discuss.

Action Research

Although many in second language education tend to treat action research as a stand-alone theory in education, it comes under the umbrella of reflective practice. Indeed, action research and reflective teaching practice are depicted as closely connected in the literature on reflective practice: action research concerns the transformation of research into action, just like any aspect of reflective practice. As Edge (2001: 8) noted, local understandings of issues are prioritized in such a way so that action researchers "communicate the perceived value of the experience-in-context." Action research has been defined variously and there are many forms, arising from different epistemological bases. For example, Bailey

(2001: 490) defines action research for language teachers as "an approach to collection and interpreting data which involves a clear, repeated cycle of procedures." The general stages (cyclical) of the action research process are: (1) plan (problem identification), (2) research (literature review), (3) observe (collecting data), (4) reflect (analysis), and (5) act (redefining the problem). The teacher sees a need to investigate a problem (perceived or otherwise) and then starts to plan how to investigate ways of solving this problem.

Wallace (1998: 21) maintains that when selecting a topic and purpose for action research, language teachers need to also consider the "why" and "what" of the topic by first seeking answers to the following questions: "Why are you engaging in this action research?"; "What area are you going to investigate?"; "What is the precise area you are going to ask yourself within that area?" These questions can narrow the focus somewhat as teachers clarify the specific purpose of the action research, and the specific topic that will be covered. The teacher may begin the process by reading some background literature on the problem to give him or her some ideas on how to approach the problem. The teacher then plans a strategy to collect data now that the problem has been identified and researched. Once the data has been collected, the teacher then analyzes and reflects on it and makes a data-driven decision to take some action. The final step in this spiraling cycle of research and action is problem redefinition. In this way, language teachers can take more responsibility for the decisions they make in their classes. However, these decisions are now informed decisions, not just based on feelings or impulse.

Teachers can also collaborate on action research projects. As Burns (1995: 5) suggests, teachers, when working collaboratively with other teachers, can "simultaneously draw on and distance themselves from their established approaches to classroom action." If teachers engage in collaborative action research projects that can also, as Burns (1999: 183) maintains, help "build a community of practitioners aligned towards teacher research and a professional climate that is open to public scrutiny and constructive critique." When teachers collaborate on action research projects this can also lead to more of a focus on conducting action research projects beyond the classroom setting to the broader society, a focus that has not had much attention in the field of TESOL. Indeed, we must remember that action research was first developed (in the United States) by Lewin (1943) as a means of addressing social issues and improving problems. This more critical approach to action research was also suggested by Elliott (1991: 69) as a type of research that could encompass society as a whole with a view to "improving the quality of action" in that society. However, within second language education, action research has usually been associated with the study of classroom actions rather than addressing social problems associated with language teaching.

Within TESOL action research has been looked at as a means of helping teachers resolve practical teaching issues and problems. However, Carr and Kemmis (1985) have suggested that action research should have a social orientation for teachers and this goes far beyond the classroom. Carr and Kemmis (1985: 220) define such an approach to action research as "a form of self-reflective enquiry" undertaken by participants in social situations in order to improve the rationality and justice of their own social or educational practices, as well as their understanding of these practices and the situations in which these practices are carried out." Within second language teaching as I have mentioned above, action research has usually been associated with classroom actions rather than addressing social problems associated with language teaching and as such will be the focus of the next chapter, "Beyond Practice."

Reflective Moment

- Decide on a topic you would like to investigate as an action research project. You can choose a topic/issue from the following ideas or you can come up with your own action research (AR) project:

  Teaching the four skills (issues related to changes in the way aspects of reading, writing, listening, or speaking are taught in your class).

  Classroom dynamics (issues related to the kinds of interaction which occur in the language classroom).

  Learner language (issues related to the kind of language that is generated by specific activities your students use when completing classroom discussions and the amount of language they produce during pair or group work).

  Grouping arrangements (issues related to how different grouping arrangements such as pair, group, or whole class, promote learner motivation, language use, and cooperation).

  Use of materials (issues relating to different ways in which materials are used and how these affect the outcomes of lessons).

  Grammar and vocabulary (issues related to the teaching of grammar and vocabulary and the effect of using different teaching and learning strategies).

  Assessment policies and techniques (issues relating to the forms of assessment you currently use in your classes and their outcomes).

- Examine each of the methods of collecting data for an action research project and considering the project you have decided to investigate in the above question, choose one or a combination of approaches for collecting data below to help you with your AR project (adapted from Burns, 1995).

  Journals/diaries: Regular dated accounts of teaching/learning plans, activities, and classroom occurrences, including personal philosophies, feelings, reactions, reflections, explanations.

  Teaching logs: More objective notes on teaching events, their objectives, participants, resources used, procedures, processes, outcomes (anticipated and unanticipated).

  Document collection: Sets of documents relevant to the research context, e.g., course overviews, lesson plans, students' writings, classroom materials/ texts, assessment tasks/texts, student profiles, student records.

Observation: Closely watching and noting classroom events, happenings, or interactions, either as a participant in the classroom (participant observer) or as an observer of another teacher's classroom (non-participant observation). Observation can be combined with field notes, recordings, and logs or journals.

Field notes: Descriptions and accounts of observed events, including non-verbal information, physical settings, group structures, interactions between participants. Notes can be time-based (e.g., every five minutes) or unstructured according to the researchers purpose.

Recording: Audio or video recordings, providing objective records of what occurred, which can be re-examined. Photographs or slides can be included.

Transcription: Written representations of verbal recordings, using conventions for identifying speakers and indicating pauses, hesitation, overlaps, and any necessary non-verbal information.

- One possible drawback of engaging in action research for a teacher and indeed in any form of reflecting on practice is that it can get in the way of teaching. How can you combine teaching and conducting an action research project at the same time?

Conclusion

Reflecting on practice is important for teachers because practice or experience alone is not enough for development; teachers must consciously process those teaching experiences by systematically reflecting on their practice. This chapter has explored how teachers can systematically reflect on practice through different lenses such as classroom observations, and through action research. Reflecting on practice through classroom observations can be done by a teacher alone or with the aid of peers through various arrangements such as peer coaching, team teaching, and lesson study. Teachers can also conduct action research projects on issues that arise from classroom observations, and concept mapping. These action research projects can be directed to resolving classroom-based issues or can be expanded beyond the classroom. This latter focus of action research is covered in the next chapter.

Chapter Reflections

- Now is a good time to compare what you say you do with what you actually do in class. In the previous chapters you have articulated your philosophy, principles, and theory of practice (theoretical foundations of practice) and in this current chapter you have examined your practice. Compare both and see whether there are any inconsistencies between your theoretical foundations of practice and your practice, or what you actually do.

8
BEYOND PRACTICE

Introduction

The first four levels/stages in the *Framework for Reflecting on Practice* that I have presented so far in this book have explored, in reverse order, practice (Chapter 7), theory (Chapter 6), principles (Chapter 5) and philosophy (Chapter 4). All of these are very much focused on reflecting on what teachers do, how they do it, why they do it, and the results of what they do. In other words it looks at the technical aspects of practice in terms of exploring teaching routines and their impact on student learning. While I think these first four levels/stages of reflecting on practice are very important, I also believe that reflecting on practice includes reflecting *beyond practice* or beyond the technical aspects of practice. I agree with Bartlett's (1990: 204) early observations on reflective practice when he saw a need to include the broader society in reflections; he suggested that in order to become truly reflective, teachers must "transcend the technicalities of teaching and think beyond the need to improve our instructional techniques." Thus, at its most basic level, reflecting *beyond practice* involves a process of "making judgments about whether professional activity is equitable, just, and respectful of persons or not" (Hatton and Smith, 1995: 35). Some have called this aspect of reflective practice critical reflection, but as you will discover in this chapter, within the field of TESOL the term has not been defined correctly with some scholars suggesting it means asking why we do (the conceptual level only) what we do in practice.

However, critical reflection encompasses the whole being of the teacher—the contemplative, reflective, cognitive, emotional, ethical, moral, social, and political aspects of our professional (and personal) lives. What transforms reflection from technical to "critical" is our ability to transform our environment (professional and personal) into something we consider equitable for all within that world, and not just the privileged few. As noted in Chapter 4 (principles) Brookfield (1995: 126) has reminded teachers that they must be on guard against "dominant or hegemonic assumptions which may influence our practice unwittingly." So this chapter introduces level/stage 5, the final level/stage of the *Framework for Reflecting on Practice* that encourages teachers to reflect *beyond practice*. One reason for reflecting beyond practice is that teachers may be able to understand the way particular societal assumptions they may have been following in their practice are in fact socially restrictive. However, through a process of reflection and critical reflection teachers can develop new ideas that can empower them to become transformative intellectuals within society. This chapter outlines and discusses critical reflection and includes a (re)definition of critical reflection to include exploring, examining, and reflecting not only on teachers' "foundational theory of practice" and practice but also the moral, political, and social issues that underlie and impact teachers' practice.

Critical Reflection

Fook and Askeland (2007), using a critical theory lens, suggest that critical reflection involves looking at the influence of the context of knowledge and power in order to be able to understand how social context influences people's assumptions and how people in turn influence these. As Fook and Askeland (2007: 3) have noted:

> Critical reflection must incorporate an understanding of personal experiences within social, cultural and structural contexts. Ultimately, through critical reflection on deep assumptions, especially about the social world and the individual person's connection with it, a person should be able to become more empowered in acting within and upon her or his social world.

In general terms critical reflection involves a process of unearthing and identifying previously unquestioned norms in society, the community, the school, and the classroom within the contexts in which they are practiced. Within the field of education, Brookfield (1995, 2006) maintains that we reflect critically for two main purposes: to better understand power relations within education and to question assumptions and practices that may seem to make our professional lives easier; however, these may actually go against our own self-interests (similar to discussions on hegemonic assumptions in Chapter 4). As Brookfield (1995, 2006) noted, classrooms are not isolated and cut off from our social and political lives and so we should become more aware of power relations. Critical reflection can help move such power relationships that are usually manifested as power *over* to become power *with* when it comes to the relationship between teachers and learners.

Thus it is important for teachers to critically reflect on practice because it helps them (adapted from Brookfield, 1995, 2006):

- *Make informed decisions and actions in teaching*: Teachers can justify (to themselves and others) their decision-making and classroom actions because they have examined the consequences (theoretically, practically, socially, and morally) of these decisions and actions.
- *Develop a rationale for practice*: Teachers, because they have intensively reflected on philosophy, principles and theory, and practice can articulate what they do, how they do it, the result of what they do. Moreover, they can now explain this rationale behind practice not only to themselves but also to colleagues and their students.
- *Avoid self-laceration*: In many previous workshops that I facilitated on reflective practice I have mentioned this self-laceration to many teachers in terms of teachers beating themselves up with the metaphorical baseball bat if they "think" something has not gone well in classes. However, if teachers critically reflect on all aspects of practice and make informed decisions about teaching, they can become less prone to self-laceration. Critically reflective teachers recognize that there is only so much they can do to prepare and try to provide a place where learning is encouraged but if students do not want to learn, then teachers should stop blaming themselves and develop an understanding that other reasons for their resistance outside the classroom conspire against them and these limit teachers' ability to change their level of resistance. This grounds teachers more emotionally.
- *Discover a voice*: Because teachers have critically reflected on practice, they can speak to others about their practice in an organized manner. They have learned from reflecting on practice and want to share this with other teachers who may not have developed their own voice. In such a manner they can not only begin to shape and transform practice but also aspects of the TESOL profession.

Closely connected to critical reflective practice within the field of second language teaching is critical applied linguistics (see also action research in previous chapter). Although I would suggest that a critical perspective within TESOL is still trying to find its center, within applied linguistics, Crookes (2009:2) maintains that "a critical perspective is no longer an 'add on,' but a perspective that has become infused into the field of applied linguistics as a whole." Crookes (1989: 51) has noted that a critical approach within TESOL is also important because second language teachers can find themselves in situations that often involve: (a) mandated and centralized curricula; (b) large amounts of administration related to accountability demands; (c) limited interaction, because of timetabling arrangements or physical location; (d) large classes and lack of resources. In order to alleviate such issues Crookes (2009) suggests TESOL teachers form their own study circles and network professionally with other teachers in other contexts and work through other teacher organizations and unions as a way of taking a more critical stance in the profession. In an interesting example of what ESL teachers can do even when they ask legislatures to help with funding, Crookes (2009: 4) came up with a set of four headings that teachers for Hawaii could consider when taking a critical stance to their practice:

1. *Organize*: Develop institutional networks, develop connections with parents, and develop networks in the community.
2. *Address leadership*: Address leadership but try to see that all are leaders, if provided with the right orientation and skills.
3. *Fundraise*: There is a literature on fundraising in education, mainly targeting the post- secondary level but little guidance for the rest of us.
4. *Engage in action*: The old slogan "direct action gets the goods" is relevant because in many places conventional politicking will not provide what a critical language teacher might need.

One final aspect related to the concept of critical reflection is teaching as a moral activity or the teaching of values and morals. As Dewey (1909: 58) noted, "every subject, every method of instruction, every incident of school life [is] pregnant with moral possibility." So if we think about the act of teaching and a teacher's integrity are we not trying to teach the "truth" to our students? I first remember seeing this reference some time ago about the first real opposition to the applied science model within teacher education from the work of Tom (1980, 1984, 1986), who viewed teaching as a type of moral craft. I have always believed that the teacher, the curricula, the school, and the community have an important influence on the moral growth of teachers and students and indeed, students in turn can influence teachers' moral growth as well. For example, we can see that teachers play an important role when choosing the content of each lesson, the way they carry themselves in their classrooms, and how they interact with, and evaluate their students. We can say that this relates to teachers' conduct both inside and outside the classroom, and as Fenstermacher (1990: 265) has noted, "the teachers' conduct at all times and in all ways is a moral matter." Within the TESOL profession the moral dimensions of teaching have not received much coverage yet language teachers deal with moral issues in their everyday teaching such as deciding which materials to use in lessons, which can impact their students' morals and their lives. Morality and teaching English to speakers of other languages has recently included the idea of religious beliefs as part of teacher knowledge (Baurain, 2012). Baurain (2012) has argued that "spiritual and religious beliefs should be part of academic conversations and research about teacher knowledge, especially because spiritual and religious beliefs already fit the area of inquiry the field has defined for itself." I will not enter this debate and instead I leave it up to each reader to decide the nature and level of the moral aspect of their practice and reflecting on practice.

Reflective Moment

- What is your understanding of the term critical reflection?
- What depth of reflection do you want to engage in and why?
- Do you think teachers should look beyond their practice and reflect on how they impact and are impacted by society?
- What are your beliefs about power relations in your classroom and where do they originate from?
- Do you have an approach to diversity in your classroom and how do you respond to diversity?
- What are the hierarchical structures and traditions within the place you teach and is collaboration with peers encouraged or discouraged?
- If collaboration is discouraged, why is this?
- If collaboration is encouraged, how is it encouraged?
- Do you think that a critical approach within TESOL is just an "add on"?
- What does critical pedagogy mean to you?
- Look at Crookes' (2009) four headings for teachers wishing to engage in a critical approach and discuss which headings are possible for you and your teaching context.
- Can you add more headings?
- What links do you perceive between your morals and/or religious beliefs and your practice?

Critical Reflection Through Dialogue

So far we have discussed the various components of critical reflection and how these impact the field of TESOL, such as a critical applied linguistics that includes a critical approach to action research (see also previous chapter), and moral (and religious) reflection. Now we will look at how the process of critical reflection can be applied within a social setting. As Kumaravadivelu (2012: 95) has argued: "Teaching is a reflective activity which at once shapes and is shaped by the doing of theorizing which in turn is bolstered by the collaborative process of dialogic inquiry." This dialogic application builds on previous work I have carried out with groups of teachers as they have reflected on their work over the years (see the introduction to this book) and as I see it, an important aspect of the *Framework for Reflecting on Practice* as presented in this book. I suggest that implementing a process of critical reflection must be a deliberative move on the part of practicing teachers if they are to take full responsibility for their own development and the development of the TESOL profession. Taking such a deliberative move is in tune with taking a critical stance if such a move involves reflecting with another group of teachers in a non-judgmental, open climate of discussion which welcomes multiple and contradictory views in a safe environment. I will discuss how such groups can operate in more detail in the next section.

Teacher Reflection Groups

As I have mentioned in the introduction to this book I started my reflective practice research as an academic working with a teacher reflection group in Seoul,
South Korea in 1994. At that time I learned a lot about the power of a group
reflecting rather than an individual teacher reflecting alone as the group became
more empowered as a result of their discussions. With the aid of the group each
teacher began to challenge themselves and each other and as a result they became
more confident teachers because they reflected on their practice (Oprandy et
al., 1999: 152). That was over 20 years ago and over the years I have continued
to work with teachers of all experiences to facilitate their reflections on their
practice.

Recently I decided to revisit teacher group reflections again and basically
repeat my dissertation by working with an experienced group of three ESL teachers in Canada as they reflected on their work (Farrell, 2014). This time I followed
my early framework (Farrell, 2004, 2007a) of reflective teaching composed of
five components: (a) a range of opportunities and activities, (b) ground rules, (c)
provision for four different times or categories of reflection, (d) external input,
and (e) trust in order to facilitate their reflections. From this research based on
the experiences of the teachers I worked with, I have learned the following about
teacher reflection groups that I hope can assist other teachers wishing to engage
in critical reflection in a teacher group.

Forming Teacher Reflection Groups

When forming such groups teachers must consider many issues such as: the type
of group they want, the number of participants to include at formation, the different roles of each participant, what to discuss, how to sustain the group, and how
to evaluate the group when the reflection period has ended.

Type of Group

When considering the type of group that ESL teachers would want to reflect
in, the overall philosophical approach to the group should be considered and
discussed. For example, although never really articulated by the members, the
overall philosophical approach to the group reported on in this book was one
of *power-with* where collaboration was emphasized and members did not impose
their interests, topics, or values on one another. Rather, they mutually fulfilled
their desires by acting together as a group rather than individuals within a group.
As Kriesberg (1992) has noted, a *power-with*-type group empowers its members
because members find ways to satisfy their desires and to fulfill their interests
without imposing these on each other. Kriesberg (1992: 85–6) continues: "The
relationships of co-agency is one in which there is equality: situations in which

individuals and groups fulfill their desires by acting together. It is jointly developing capacity." T1, who was a member of a teacher reflection group, noted after the period of reflection that, "It seemed to me that we wanted to find topics of mutual interest to pursue and discuss where the group could go forward together as one." The alternative type of group is *power-over* characterized by command and control (by members or a facilitator), but as Kriesberg (1992: 47) also notes, a power-over relationship "cuts off human communication and creates barriers to human empathy and understanding." Therefore, all the members in the teacher reflection group must be willing to commit to the support of one another's reflective practices if it is to be an empowering experience for each member. Once this issue is discussed and agreed upon, the teacher reflection group can consider where they want to draw their members from and how many members they want in it.

Previously I have outlined (see Farrell, 2007) three main types of teacher reflection groups and they can extend not only within the school but may span several schools or school districts as well as other organizations: *peer groups* can be set up within a school, *teacher groups* can be set up at the district level, *district level groups*, and *virtual groups* that can be formed anywhere. The teacher reflection group formation reported on in this paper comes under peer groups (a group with their colleagues in the same institution), and as one participant suggested, the ideal number should be no more than four, which was "enough for a group because there was always the concern about one person dominating the conversation" (T1). Once a group of teachers decide that they want to form a teacher reflection group they must then figure out how they want to operate such a group in terms of general rules, participants' roles, and topic setting. When deciding what type of group to form, teachers must be aware of two different types of groups: power-with and power-over groups.

Reflective Moment

- What is your understanding of a *power-with*-type group?
- What is your understanding of a *power-over*-type group?
- What type of teacher reflection group would you like to set up and why?
- How would you set it up?
- Groups need a clear purpose; where it involves learning, the aims, objectives, and outcomes should be explicit. How would you establish the purpose of your group?

Forming the Group

Richardson (1997) has suggested that when colleagues come together in a group to reflect on their work, four basic features or ingredients need to be present if the group is to be successful:

- Each participant needs to feel "safe" within the group. In the teacher reflection group I worked with recently one teacher commented: "My colleagues are also my friends and I feel extremely comfortable sharing my thoughts with them."
- Each participant needs to feel "connected" in some way or other. In the teacher reflection group I worked with recently one teacher commented: "The group provided time to share common experiences, ask for or offer insights and advice, and ponder solutions."
- Each participant has to have a sense and to be able to feel passionate about the group and what they are trying to accomplish together. In the teacher reflection group I worked with recently one teacher later reflected: "Face to face discussion was important for bonding the group and renewing our commitment to the process each week."
- Each participant must honor, and be grateful for the group's existence. In the teacher reflection group I worked with recently one teacher noted that: "It was nice to be able to affirm and support each other as we expressed concerns or doubts, too."

As can be seen from the teachers' comments, the above four features were important for defining the group's existence for the participants in the case study reported in this paper because they sought out each other (and the facilitator) for the camaraderie of working together as a teacher reflection group. Thus, such teacher reflection groups should offer moral support where vulnerabilities are shared and aired in a safe environment. Risk taking should also be encouraged in such groups, where self-confidence is enhanced by positive encouragement and feedback for each of the group members. That said, group members should not just validate everything each member says about their practice simply because a member said it. In fact, this was probably the biggest weakness of the teacher reflection group reported on in this book because the members tended to agree mostly with all the group comments and there was little challenging of other member's comments. In the teacher reflection group I worked with recently one teacher noted after the period of reflection:

> I don't think we were especially critical of each other. We tended not to challenge or disagree. Our long-term professional relationship and friendship is too precious to risk. I think we tended to question or judge ourselves more harshly and then the other two would rush in to say—don't be so hard, or to support what the teacher had done. However, we did give examples of how we do things differently and provided alternatives through anecdotal experiences of our own.

Teacher reflection groups must be on guard against overly romanticizing the teacher's voice; rather, such groups should also be a place where constructive criticism and even conflict is welcomed because such critical dialogue can be a necessary catalyst for any change.

Reflective Moment

- How would you cover the four basic features listed above for forming a group?
- People in groups should be given the opportunity to make their expectations explicit. This helps to identify whether these are realistic. How will you deal with this issue?
- People need to know for how long the group will be working and meeting. How will you deal with this issue?
- Why is risk taking important for a teacher reflection group?
- Why would conflict lead to change?
- Why should group members not just validate everything another member says in a group?
- Why should groups be on guard against overly romanticizing the teacher's voice?
- How can groups deal with the following issues when starting:
  - o   Confidentiality
  - o   Giving constructive criticism
  - o   Not attacking, or putting down others
  - o   Expressing feelings
  - o   Observing time keeping
  - o   Honesty
  - o   Listening to others
  - o   Only one person to speak at a time
  - o   Asking questions of clarity
  - o   Right to keep silent
  - o   Acceptance of the diversity of individuals within the group
  - o   Sexist, racist language will not be tolerated
  - o   Inclusive language to be used throughout

Group Roles

Each teacher reflection group will be composed of members with different roles, one of the most important being the group's leader. I would suggest a democratic approach to discussions, where nobody attempts to manipulate the group into doing what he or she wants. It may also be possible for a teacher reflection group to have a type of co-existing leadership in order to provide more opportunities for getting the task done (one co-leader) and maintaining group cohesion (another co-leader). When groups come together they go through developmental stages that can see changes in their roles and this is especially true if they have a facilitator to help the group reflect. I was a facilitator for all the teacher groups I worked with and I found at the beginning that I was making most of the decisions about the content of the group discussions and the way the group would operate. However, as the group members became more at ease and confident this locus of control began shifting to other individuals within the group and with this last group of teachers I noted that all of the decision making rested entirely with the group itself towards the end of the reflective process. So, groups should note that effective facilitators should enable group members to take more control of the process as the group gains more experience talking to and interacting with each other. During the group discussions the three teachers tended to take on roles although they were not conscious of these roles. For example, in the teacher reflection group I worked with recently one teacher took on the role of *team worker* because she was always trying to cement the group together and also the role of *implementer* as she was always there to see that things were completed. The other two teachers also took on these roles but to a lesser extent. Another teacher took on the role of *monitor* because she wanted to ensure that all opinions and options were considered. The third teacher took on the role of *listener* as she was the most silent of the three.

Reflective Moment

- Discuss each role above.
- How can you handle some of the following issues related to roles that may occur in your group:
  o   Bids for leadership?
  o   Overdependence on the facilitator?
  o   Feeling left out with no role?
  o   Subgroups that develop with their own roles?
  o   People who are quietly subversive by saying nothing?
- What other roles do you think would be necessary in your group?

Modes of Reflection

Once the group has discussed and agreed on the allocation of different roles for the period of reflection, they should then consider what opportunities they will provide for reflection. For example, the teacher reflection groups I have worked with decided to use group discussions to aid their reflections in combination with regular journal writing, and some classroom observations of each other's lessons. To accomplish this each group had to come up with some ground rules to decide each activity or mode or reflection and within the activity about what to do and how to do it. Consequently, each group will have to discuss and agree on the number of group meetings they can commit to during the period of their reflection as well as if and when they will all write in their teacher journal, and if and when they will observe each other teach. The teacher reflection group members all seemed to like and benefit from the combination of talking, writing, and observing rather than focusing on any one of these modes of reflection. Most groups try to use a combination of group discussion, journal writing, and classroom observations and as one teacher in the group I worked with recently noted:

> I liked the cycle and interplay between the realities of my classroom and workplace, the journal, the discussion group and then small classroom research or PD activities. Any of them on their own would have been "ok" but together they really enriched the experience. It was a full experience. I got to study my classroom and students; reflect upon myself as a teacher (quite specifically and holistically); and feel supported by my colleagues and learn from them (including the facilitator).

Of course, other teacher reflection groups may want to consider other modes of reflection and adjust the three talked about above to their own particular setting and needs.

Reflective Moment

- What is your preference for a mode of reflection from talking, writing, and/ or observing?
- Which mode would be easiest for you and why?
- Which mode would be difficult for you and why?
- Can you think of any other mode of reflection that would be suitable for you and your group?

Discussion Topics

When teacher reflection groups come together for the first time they may or may not have a focus for the group discussions. The recent teacher reflection group I worked with did not have any particular topics in mind from the beginning, so they just let topics emerge and develop from their teaching and discussions at that time. In addition, the group did not have any other similar group to compare with nor did they have a list of topics they could consider. So, other groups may want to first brainstorm a theme or topic together and then narrow it down by identifying specific questions to explore. This narrowing down of a topic allows participants to focus their attention on issues that have personal meaning for them. The group can also at this stage decide if they have the resources available for them to continue reflecting on that particular topic. When the topic is temporarily exhausted, then the group can start another cycle of brainstorming a topic followed by a narrowing of the topic with development of specific questions addressing that topic.

Reflective Moment

- Would you discuss the topics mentioned above?
- What other topics would you want to discuss in your group?
- Brookfield (2006) came up with two ideas to get group discussions started: a "reflective inventory" and a "personal assumption inventory" Examine and discuss each of these and see if they are suitable for your group:
  - o *Reflective inventory*: Participants take turns introducing themselves by answering six simple questions:
    What am I proudest of in my work as a teacher?
    What would I like my students to say about me when I'm out of the room?
    What do I most need to learn about in my teaching?
    What do I worry most about in my work as a teacher?
    When do I know I've done good work?
    What's the mistake I've made and learned the most from? Another exercise is a
  - o *Personal assumptions inventory*: participants first complete the following sentences and then share with the group:
    I know I've done good work when . . .
    I know I've done bad work when . . .
    I feel best about my work when . . .
    I feel worst about my work when . . .
    The last time I saw really good teaching was when . . .
    The best learning experience I've ever seen students involved in was when . . .

Sustaining the Group

In order to sustain any teacher reflection group each member must be committed to the group. The teacher reflection group I worked with recently lasted for one semester intensively and another semester intermittently. For the first semester, the group met each Saturday morning for one or two hours to reflect on their work. Commitment for intensive reflection with a group of teachers should last ideally for one semester according to the teachers reported on in this paper. Although the beginning of this teacher reflection group was shaky in terms of commitment, when they all realized the benefits of the reflective process, they all made the most of these meetings. As one teacher noted in her post-group reflections: "I admit that when we first talked about giving up Saturday morning I felt a bit concerned about whether I had made the right choice but in the end felt it was time well spent." Because teaching is a very personal activity, as teachers in a reflection group begin to open up and discuss professional (and personal) issues that are important to them with other teachers whom they may or may not know, there will inevitably be a certain level of anxiety present. So a non-threatening environment of trust should be fostered in the group. Although trust was not an issue in the teacher reflection group I worked with recently because the teachers had been colleagues and friends for over 15 years, one teacher did mention it in her post-group reflections: "I think that establishing trust is the key factor in creating an environment that supports cooperative discussion and reflection." Ways of establishing trust can be incorporated into the reflective process itself, such as emphasizing description and observation over judgment in group discussions as was the case in the group I worked with recently.

Linked to the idea of establishing trust in a group is the issue of emotion. Because teacher groups are composed of individual humans reflecting on various aspects of their practice different feelings and emotions will inevitably surface during the life of the group, such as fear, anger, frustration, enjoyment, safety, warmth, insecurity, boredom. Indeed, individual members will have different ways of showing their emotions and of course different ways of hiding such emotions depending on the cultural context of the meetings. So it is important that the group establish early on in the reflective process that they respect the right of individual group members not to disclose their feelings if they do not want to and as Brookfield (1995: 9) has cautioned, sitting in a large circle may not help this process as people may have the feeling of "having nowhere to hide." Each group will have to decide how they want to deal with emotions that arise in group discussions.

Reflective Moment

- How can you plan for sustaining your group?
- Do you think having a set period for reflections will help sustain the group?
- How will you approach the issue of trust in the group?
- How can you establish group trust?
- People deal with emotions in different ways. Discuss the following ways some teachers have handled their emotions:
  Responsibility for emotions by "owning" them
  Storing up emotions
  Assertiveness and the expression of emotions

Evaluating the Group

After a teacher reflection group concludes its period of reflection it is important that all group participants evaluate the influences of the group on their personal and professional growth so that they can have some closure. Participants can reflect on whether they achieved their individual and group goals, their individual accomplishments and the group's accomplishments and factors that can be considered if they or others want to set up another teacher development group. As one teacher reflected after her group experiences: "We shared what was happening in our classrooms and professional lives and I don't think we found solutions per se, but I think we provided a forum for each of us as individuals to articulate what was happening and then to share similar experiences in a supportive way." Also they can at this stage consider if they want to share their findings with other teachers who may benefit from hearing about their experiences. They can attend a conference and report about their group to other teachers and they can also write up the group developments for a journal publication. This is an example of critical reflective practice outlined earlier in this chapter. The participants in the group I worked with recently became engaged with their community when they presented their experiences of participating in such a teacher reflection group at a teacher conference. One of the teachers in the group reported at the conference that she had a positive experience with her group: "I think this experience has given me the confidence, skills, and motivation to continue this type of professional development in the future and to enjoy my teaching in this new phase of my career that I feel is coming up."

Reflective Moment

- How will you evaluate the success of your teacher reflection group?
- Do you think that in order to be truly critically reflective teachers must go to conferences and share their experiences with other teachers, administrators, and others who work in educating second language learners? Why or why not?

Conclusion

This chapter has presented the final stage of the *Framework for Reflecting on Practice*: beyond practice. This important stage of the framework has outlined and discussed the importance of critical reflective practice and how this impacts the field of TESOL in critical applied linguistics, sociocultural theory, and moral and religious reflective practice. In addition, the chapter has suggested that the process of critical reflection is best carried out with other teachers in a teacher reflection group. It is important, however, to detail how such groups can be formed and to discuss such issues as the type of group teachers want to form, the different roles group members will take on, their preferred modes of reflection, the topics they want to discuss, how they will sustain the group, and also how they will evaluate the group after the period of critical reflection.

Chapter Reflections

- Now that you have completed the cycle of reflections presented in the *Framework for Reflecting on Practice* and you have reflected on what you hold to be important to you as a reflective practitioner, write a letter to a trusted colleague articulating what reflective practice means to you. Try to make sure your colleague, whom you trust, will understand what it means to you to be a reflective practitioner.

9
NAVIGATING THE FRAMEWORK

Introduction

By outlining and describing the *Framework for Reflecting on Practice* presented in this book I have attempted to provide a holistic reflective practice tool that can help teachers at all levels of experiences with their professional development. This final chapter outlines and discusses how teachers with different levels of experience can navigate and apply the framework in a holistic manner from whatever perspective they think will further their professional development aims as teachers of English to speakers of other languages. I also provide two case study examples of ESL teachers at different stages of their careers as they attempt to apply the model to their professional development needs.

Navigating the Framework

The *Framework for Reflecting on Practice* depicted in this book as a promising professional development tool that can guide TESOL teachers' practices regardless of the level of their experiences can be navigated in three different ways: theory-into-(beyond) practice, (beyond practice-into-theory or a single stage application. Thus it is a descriptive rather than a prescriptive framework. As mentioned in Chapter 3, teachers can take a deductive approach to reflecting on practice by moving from theory-into-practice or from stage/level 1, philosophy, through the different stages to stage/level 5, beyond practice. Some may say that pre-service teachers who do not have much classroom experience, would be best suited to take such an approach because they can first work on their overall philosophical approach to teaching English to speakers of other languages and work their way through the different stages of principles (stage/level 2), theory (stage/level 3) when they reach the practicum stage, they will be well placed then to reflect on their practice (stage/level 4) and eventually move beyond practice (stage/level 5).

This theory-driven approach to practice where philosophy and theory have an initial influence on practice is probably a natural sequence of development for novice teachers because they do not have much teaching experience. When their early practices are observed, it is most likely that theory can be detected in their practice; however, over time, and with reflection, it is possible that their everyday practice will begin to inform and even change their philosophy and theory and they may come up with new principles of practice. Thus continued reflection can nourish both practice and theory of practice. Experienced teachers too can also choose to begin their reflections at stage/level 1, philosophy, especially if they consider their philosophy as a significant basis of their practice with principles second, theory third and so on through the framework. Experienced teachers, some of whose practice can be theory-driven if they have been reading and experimenting with applications of particular theories throughout their teaching careers, most likely describe their work in terms of their overall philosophical approach to teaching English to speakers of other languages and this description probably embeds a lot of their values, beliefs, principles, and theories behind their practice. When such teachers are observed teaching their lessons, we are likely to see that their approaches, methods, and activities often reflect the influence of these theories. An example of this is where a teacher takes a science/research conceptual approach to their teaching and attempts to implement task-based language teaching approaches (TBLT) into their lessons.

Theory-into-(Beyond) Practice

The following outlines a short case study of how one novice ESL teacher in his first year of teaching attempted to incorporate strategy training when teaching English reading classes to ESL students in a high school. He attempted to teach reading strategy training in his classes from the start of the semester because he said they were "taught this idea in my teacher preparation program." He was especially interested in teaching his students the learning strategies of questioning, clarifying, and predicting as well as vocabulary recognition techniques to less proficient ESL students many of whom were struggling with their reading comprehension and as a result did not like to read in English.

We started with a discussion of his philosophy of practice and the novice teacher stated: "I have a definite philosophy of teaching: I think that all students always come first. If a particular program or course of action will benefit them, I will try to carry it out. If it's not going to benefit the students, I will try to scrap it or play it down." He said that much of his approach to practice will have this philosophy as an underlying influence although he also realized that he had no real teaching experience and his practicum experience was only him observing others teach, so he said that he did not really get any ideas from that experience.

He was especially interested in teaching reading to struggling ESL students because he said that he felt this was his "calling" or vocation as a teacher (see Chapter 4 for more on "teaching as a calling"). He said that he was not really interested in teaching students who were excellent as he said that they would probably not benefit much from his knowledge and that was not why he got into teaching. So he asked me to observe his teaching of reading rather than any other language skill. He said that his beliefs about learning and teaching reading centered around learner strategy training that he had studied in his teacher education program and he believed that if you teach ESL struggling readers how to use strategies such as prediction, questioning, and clarifying they would become better readers. I observed five of his reading classes: two at the start of the second semester, two in the middle of the semester, and one near the end of the semester. Each observation covered two double periods of 40 minutes for each period except for the final observation which was one 40-minute class. Excerpts from each of the lessons are provided. These excerpts (in the form of episodes) show how the teacher attempted to incorporate strategy training into his teaching of English reading. The teacher authenticated the episodes and the interpretations that follow.

Observed Lessons Start of Semester

These lessons were conducted at the start of the second week of the semester. The first lesson started with the teacher stating that he was going to review reading comprehension methods. In this lesson the teacher tried to get his students to think and reflect about how they usually read and how they answer reading comprehension questions after reading a text. First, the teacher took the students through what he called "the traditional steps for answering ten reading comprehension questions" because he noted his students were used to this and also how the students seemed to not be able to answer most of the questions. Then he attempted to introduce the learning strategy of prediction (that he learned in his teacher education program) while they are reading.

The following dialogue, as outlined in episode 1, shows how the teacher tried to introduce the strategy of prediction and how the class responded. The teacher makes a reference to "this usual way on comprehension" in the first line indicating that in traditional English reading classes in his context, the students are asked to read a passage, underline any words they do not understand, and then answer the comprehension questions that follow the passage. The teacher then checks the answers and informs the students whether they are correct or not. He was trying to break this cycle.

Episode 1

T: *Which students don't follow this usual way of comprehension?*
[Most hands went up]
T: *Today another method . . . try and guess what is going to happen in a story.*
[The teacher writes the title of the story "The Last Dance" on board]
T: *What is the first thing that comes to mind?* [No answers].
T: *What will the story be about?* [No answers]
T: *Read the first paragraph.*
T: *Now what do you think the story is or will be about?*
[Teacher asks more questions about the first paragraph; no student able to answer].
[The teacher then asked the students about their metacognitive skills]
T: *What happens in your mind? Thinking, predicting.*
[No reaction from any student]
T: *What is the next paragraph going to be about? Read like this.*
[Students read]
Key: **T** = teacher

This short exchange in episode 1 shows how the teacher was trying to get his students to think about their reading strategies and to consider using the strategy of prediction that he had learned during his teacher education program. However, the reality of the classroom and students he was teaching made him quickly realize that it was not going to be easy to introduce this strategy. Indeed, after this class he told me that he felt frustrated that his students were not responding to the idea of predicting while reading in the way he had hoped and that this was different to what he expected from his theory classes while he was training.

Nonetheless, he said that he saw some hope as the students had told him that they had never been asked about how they read (their reading strategies) before. They said they were usually told to read the passage silently (or aloud) and answer the comprehension questions. Thus, the teacher said that at least he got some response and that some of the students were becoming curious about what the teacher was trying to do. Consequently, he said that he would continue with strategy training as the students needed a new approach because they had failed to comprehend passages so often before in classes he had observed while he was on teaching practice and during his first year of teaching.

Observed Lessons Mid-Semester

These lessons took place in the middle of the second semester. The teacher told me before this class that he had continued with strategy training since my last visit, especially the strategy of prediction for reading lessons. However, he said that he had not incorporated it into every reading lesson since the first set of lessons because he noticed the students were not responding. The class started with the teacher asking the students to read a passage silently. After 10 minutes of silent reading he asked the students to reflect on their learning as outlined in the following dialogue in episode 2.

Episode 2

T: *How many used predicting? [Three students raised their hands]*
T: *The rest of you . . . how many read each word?* [All students raised their hands]
T: *I advise you to try the new methods. I can't force you but you will find it easier to answer comprehension questions. I know it works. Try it and you have a choice.*
Key: **T** = teacher

Again this short example in episode 2 shows how difficult it was for the teacher as he said, "to break the old habits of traditional reading approaches" especially for less proficient ESL readers. After class the teacher said he was disappointed again that the students had not used the "new" technique but that he would keep trying. He said that he noticed a degree of resistance and he said, "Old habits die hard." He continued: "It may be that weak readers tend to lock themselves into a pattern or cycle of self-doubt about their inability to read and that they cannot easily break from this." The teacher noticed that the students were using their fingers to guide their eyes across the page and he interpreted this physical act as further evidence that they were reading word for word. He also said that the students gave up easily if they encountered vocabulary they did not understand, if they did not understand the first sentence of a passage or paragraph, or if they could not answer the first comprehension question. In fact, they equated failure (and mental pain) with the act of reading. The teacher remarked that the students in his class had always "groaned loudly" when he had told them that they were about to do a reading in English class.

So at the mid-semester point the teacher began to question the validity of his beliefs about strategy training for struggling ESL readers as he said he wondered now whether or not these strategies would in fact be useful or not for his students. He also worried that his classes may now have become boring for his students because he was trying to teach these new strategies. Up to this mid-semester point the teacher said that he had attempted strategy training in questioning, clarifying (however, he did not give me any examples of how he taught these two strategies and I do not know how much time he spent on this strategy training), and predicting strategies with not much success. He said that from this mid-semester on he would slow down and try to reinforce strategies already introduced. By this he said he meant that he would try to develop activities and exercises that would reinforce the strategies.

Observed Lesson End-Semester

I then observed a class near the end of the semester. Before the class the teacher said he was a bit frustrated with the slow uptake of any of the reading strategies he had tried to teach the class because he said that the students had resisted many of them even though they could still not answer any of the 10 or so comprehension questions that he sometimes asked in the usual "traditional way." However, he pointed out that he was beginning to get them to predict "a bit when reading" but that it was very slow and also hard work for him to keep pushing them to try to predict while they were reading. Episode 3 outlines part of the transcript of his attempts to get his students to predict once at the beginning of his lesson and again in the middle of the lesson.

Episode 3

T: *Today we will try to predict again . . . Not reading. Here is the title. What do you think the story will be about? [Nearly all students raised hands. Teacher then chooses some students to answer and they give opinion]*

[15 minutes later students read first paragraph of story]

T: *Don't worry about what kinds of words you don't know yet . . . only what type of passage it is. How many bothered about difficult words?* [Four hands raised—class of 40]

T: *Are all the details important?*

Ss: [Most shout] *No!*

T: *What is important then?*

Ss: [Most shout] *To guess what the story is about.*

T: *Yes, to predict.*

Key: **T** = teacher; **Ss** = students

Episode 3 shows how the teacher had to continually remind his students to try to predict what a reading would be about as they read and how this was always trying to remind them how important it was to have some strategy when reading. The teacher realized that it would take time to get his students to implement any reading strategies and so at the end of the semester he noted that he would have to spend time the following semester "pushing reading strategies" but that it would not be easy.

Reflective Moment

*   As you read through the reflections of this novice ESL teacher during his first semester teaching reading to struggling ESL readers, what do you notice about his overall approach to reflecting on his teaching? Would you say it is theory-driven or practice-driven?
*   Do you think his practice reflected his philosophy?

- What do you think his principles were?
- Do you think his practice was informed by his theory? If yes, how will it be informed? If not, why not?
- Do you think he will adjust his philosophy, theory, principles, and/or practices in the following semester and years? If yes, how do you think he will adjust these? If no, why not?

(Beyond) Practice-into-Theory

Teachers can also decide to reverse the process outlined above and take a more inductive approach to using the framework by moving from (beyond) practice into theory if they consider their practice (both inside and outside the classroom) as powerful determinants of their overall approach to reflecting on practice. For such an approach to the framework, teachers would first consider some issue from beyond practice (stage/level 5) or decide on a starting point from some issue within their classroom that they want to explore and then work their way through the different stages/levels in reverse order than for a deductive approach. After moving through the different stages/levels this practice-into-theory approach eventually asks teachers to examine how their practice is influenced by their philosophy or how their philosophy examines their practice when they arrive at stage/level 1 reflection. Pre-service teachers may have difficulties taking such an approach when they first begin their teacher education programs if they have not had any teaching experience through the practicum or otherwise. However, once they begin their practicum there is no reason why they cannot take such an approach to see how, for example, a critical incident that occurs while teaching is influenced by their theory, principles, and philosophy and how these in turn influence their practices both inside and outside the classroom. In such an inductive approach of moving from beyond practice into theory a teacher can select an incident from their practice that has significance for them and reflect on its meaning. Reflection on such teacher-generated critical incidents can provide information that allows teachers to reflect on how they got where they are today in their practice, how they conduct their practice, the thinking and problem-solving they employ during their practice (or their reflection-in-action that can give clues to their instructional decisions during practice), and their underlying philosophy, assumptions, values, beliefs, theories, and principles that have ruled their current and past practices. In addition, by articulating their critical incidents to themselves and others, teachers can not only reflect on the specific incidents within their teaching world, but also feel a sense of cathartic relief as it offers an outlet for tensions, feelings, and frustrations about practice that are often carried out in isolation from other teachers.

The following teacher narrative, as told (in the teacher's own words) by an experienced ESL teacher outlines the details of a critical incident that can be identified as "negative feedback" (Farrell, 2007a). McCabe's (2002) framework for analyzing the narrative that the critical incident emerged from was used as follows:

- *Orientation*: This part answers the following questions: Who? When? What? Where?
- *Complication*: Outlines what happened and the problem that occurred along with any turning point in the story.
- *Evaluation*: This part answers the question: So what? What this means for the participants in the story.
- *Result*: This part outlines and explains the resolution to the problem/crisis.

Specifically, the incident details her concerns of the "negative feedback" she reported that she received from one of her students after one of her classes. The information about the critical incident comes from a combination of teacher journal entries the teacher wrote and what she reported about the incident to the other teachers in the teacher reflection group during a group meeting. The narrative is presented in the teacher's own words so as to provide as much reality as possible.

Orientation

"I was teaching a course on Teaching English as a Second Language; most were university graduates who wanted to become ESL/EFL teachers. The survey is called the Key Performance Indicators (KPI) and it is done across the province by all colleges. It is the primary source of information about the course and we are held accountable for the responses. For example, in previous years, there was a very low part of our KPIs related to college facilities and we, as a department, had to hold a focus group discussion with our students to better understand their responses. We discussed it with our program advisory committee, and the program chair had to come up with strategies for improvement. It asks students to comment on a very wide range of things from the actual learning experience and program quality to college resources, facilities, technology, cafeteria/bookstore, skills for future career, right down to teacher punctuality. They complete it at the end of the program. Not all courses in a program have to do it every term and not all programs necessarily do one every year. Because it is so extensive, they take a cross section of programs in the college (I think). It is the type where a statement is given and the students can mark their answer on a continuum: Agree strongly, agree, neither agree nor disagree, disagree, disagree strongly (something like that)

The student in this incident was one who had repeatedly, from the very first class demonstrated a contemptuous boredom with the program as a whole. He had indicated this in a number of ways to all his teachers. In person, he was tactfully polite, but in his written assignments, he would express his truer feelings. He always seemed to resist or think he was above what we were teaching in the program. He had just completed university and seemed to think he was above a college program; although, this is now my own perception, as I seek to understand why someone would stay in a program that he clearly didn't like. Because the negative feedback came from this student, I could have dismissed it more easily. . . it was predictable;

of course he didn't like anything. It was really not a surprise. And yet, I still felt the sting of the negative result and comments and had to reflect upon why."

Complication

"When we did our official surveys and I could tell from, you know how they give you the bar graph or the percentages showing, you know disagreed, neutral, and then agree. Seven percent were always that disagree, which indicates out of a class of 19 students that one person hated everything."

Evaluation

"I was very disturbed by some unsolicited comments from the student at the end of the semester. Even after all our talk about feedback from students and our ability to take feedback and make changes, and not taking it personally, I was amazed by my hugely, negative, emotional response to his comments even though I kind of knew he was going to make them. Just when you think you're above the fray, then you get some negative feedback that hits you between the eyes. After doing some thinking on these experiences, I have come to realize that it wasn't the comment itself that disturbed me (basically because I knew it was not valid), but the fact that this student felt he had a right to criticize the course content (and indirectly me) despite the fact that he had not attended a significant portion of the course, did not try when he attended class, and actually failed the final exam. The fact is that I felt vulnerable. I think I was worried that someone (other teachers?) was going to listen to this guy and that judgments would be made about this course and about me and my teaching."

Result

"Now that I have told my story and had time to reflect, I'm totally over it. In fact, I think I am probably a more severe critic of myself than anyone else could be. I wasn't concerned by the positives or the negatives or the neutrals. I mean, I looked at them and it was interesting and there were not really surprising things but I knew that was him and it was like, oh well."

Reflection

As mentioned in Chapter 5, critical incidents that teachers choose to reflect on can be positive and/or negative events, or a "teaching high" or "teaching low" (Thiel, 1999). The incident reported on here could be classified as a teaching "low" for the teacher because the negative comments provided by the student went beyond what the teacher was expecting. As such the self-reflective critical incident outlined in the case study demonstrates how real practices (also note the use of the teacher's own words throughout) can conflict with expectations and outcomes that may necessitate a re-examination of a teacher's philosophy, theory, principles, and even practices as the teacher explores the deep meaning of such an incident. As McCabe (2002: 83) notes, when we begin to analyze such critical incidents in which outcomes conflict with our expectations, "we can come to a greater understanding of the expectations themselves—what our beliefs, philosophies, understandings, conceptions (of the classroom, of the language, of the students, of ourselves) actually are." So by recalling and describing such critical incidents in as much detail as possible, teachers can begin to explore all kinds of assumptions that underlie their practice. Research suggests that teachers who are better informed about their teaching are also better able to evaluate what aspects of their practice they may need to adjust because they are more aware of what stage they have reached in their professional development (Richards & Lockhart, 1994).

Reflective Moment

- Why do you think the teacher felt vulnerable?
- By reflecting and analyzing the critical incident outlined above, the teacher gained a greater awareness of herself as a teacher and her practices, which is one of the main goals of reflective practice. What kind of awareness of her philosophy, theory, and principles in particular do you think the teacher examined as a result of her articulating the critical incident?

Single Stage Reflections

Another way the *Framework for Reflecting on Practice* can be used by teachers regardless of their experience is to choose to reflect at only one particular stage/level. Teachers can stop reflecting at that one stage/level or they can decide to move up or down the framework and reflect at other levels as well. Teachers can decide, for example, to weave in and out of various stages/levels depending on their interests or needs at a particular time and also depending on the amount of time they have to reflect. For example, teachers may decide to start their reflections on their principles at stage/level 2 and then move to theory at level 3 and then move to their practice (level 4), or they may start at level 1 philosophy and then move to level 5 beyond practice if they have some issues that they need to address specifically at these levels. In fact, some may say that teaching does not follow any linear and ordered moves up or down these stages/levels and so a lack of order may reflect true practice.

Here is an example of a case study of a teacher who begins her reflections at one particular stage/level and moves onto other stages/levels after that. An ESL teacher with seven years teaching experience decided to begin her reflections on her principles (level/stage 2) and specifically her use of metaphors for the teacher, or "a teacher is a_____?" and fill in the blank with a critical friend. She noted that she always considered the teacher as a facilitator and wanted to examine its true meaning for her as an ESL teacher. She did not have any framework in mind to help her reflect on this so working with a critical friend, they both decided to first try and find meaning for this metaphor.

When discussing the meaning of this metaphor for the reality of TESOL, they discovered that a teacher as facilitator means that the teacher should encourage learner self-expression and autonomy and the students must be encouraged to take on the responsibility for their own learning. They also noted that their teaching methodology should be considered learner-centered and in terms of language use in the class, meaning is emphasized over accuracy. Most of the activities chosen by the teacher must also have some kind of negotiation of meaning. In terms of the content to be covered, they noted that it should not be pre-packaged; rather it should be negotiated with their students and evolve during the course. So armed with this information, the critical friend observed her teaching to see if this teacher was in fact a facilitator as outlined above.

Lesson Observation

According to the teacher the topic of the class discussion is having the students make facts and opinion statements. The teacher said before class that she wants her students to practice speaking in English regardless of the number of mistakes. She said that she hopes to teach students how to speak English fluently rather than to get them to speak accurately in terms of correct grammar. The transcript excerpt shows the opening turns of the class.

Excerpt 1

T: *Today we are going to practice speaking factual statements and opinion statements in English. Let's start with Brendan. What do you know about a fact statement?*

Brendan: A fact is true.

T: True. A true statement is a fact statement. Anyone else would like to add on to that explanation? Susan?

Susan: Will happen.

T: Will happen, hmm. Fact means something that is true. Anyone else? Peter?

Peter: Are they things that has happened before?

T: Things that have happened before. Ok. How about opinion? Who knows what the meaning of opinion is? John?

John: To ask your thinking on something.

| T: | To ask your thinking on something? Hmm . . . How about Paul? What do you . . .what you understand? |

T: To ask your thinking on something? Hmm . . . How about Paul? What do you . . .what you understand?

Paul: What you think about something is an opinion?

T: What you think about something is an opinion? How about Sally?

Sally: Things that is not true

T: Opinion means things that is not true. Sally, can you give me an example?

Sally: I think American movies not good . . . I like.

T: You think that American movies are not good. Ok. But do you mean the opposite? What I want to know is . . . is this your real opinion or do you like American movies?

Sally: No, I like. I like.

T: So, Sally, you say you like watching American movies. This is your opinion, yes?

Sally: Yes, I like American movies . . . good action scene.

T: You like American movies because there is good action in them?

Sally: Yes.

T: Ok. Any other opinions on American movies?

Reflective Moment

- In this case study the teacher started at stage/level 2 (principles) and then jumped to stage/level 4 (practice) after discussing the meaning of her metaphor of teacher as facilitator and then compared the metaphor use to the reality of her classroom lesson as outlined in the transcript above.
  - o Based on the details in the transcript do you think the teacher is a facilitator? Why or why not?
  - o Do you think the teacher's principles converge or diverged from her practice? Why or why not?

The teacher established at the beginning of the class that her focus was on meaning rather than grammatical structure of fact and opinion statements, so we can probably say from this short excerpt that there was a match between the teacher's focus and the students' perceptions of the lesson's focus. We can also probably say that there is a convergence between this teacher's principles and her actual classroom practices and she is most likely a facilitator as she has stated. Turns 1 to 21 shows the teacher is looking for meaning rather than enforcing grammatical accuracy in her students' responses, thus exhibiting a teacher as facilitator role.

The three examples outlined above suggests that for the purposes of reflecting on practice, it really does not matter where a teacher begins his or her reflections on the framework presented in this book as there are benefits regardless of the starting point of the reflections. The main point is that the *Framework for Reflecting on Practice* is a very useful professional development tool that can help teachers at all levels of experience to reflect on their practice and beyond practice and their hidden philosophy, principles, and theory behind those practices in any order they choose so that they can determine how well all are aligned. This in my opinion is *holistic reflective practice*.

Final Reflections

It is a widely held view now in teacher education and development programs that the role of reflection and the concept of teacher as "reflective practitioner" have become an accepted level of attainment for pre-service and in-service teachers. Although reflective practice has become widely promoted any review of the literature on reflection still seems to yield a somewhat bewildering terminology, a confusing range of models, levels, strategies, and even a vastly competing range of applications of reflection. I suggest that all these competing models and applications of reflective practice show how complex the concept of reflection is and how little we know about the issues associated with reflective practice. I also believe that this shows a healthy need to discuss and debate these issues, which is after all at the heart of reflecting on practice. Jay and Johnson (2002: 84) have referred to reflection as an "evolving concept" and like all other evolutions debate about its structure will be continuous—after all are we not just practicing what we are preaching by critically debating its meaning and complexity? The complexity of reflective practice is further apparent through the various attempts at defining the "critical" within critical reflection and the need to have dialogue with others rather than reflecting alone. The dominant view of reflective practice, however, that most educators agree on is that it can benefit our professional development.

Regarding their professional development most teachers realize after some time in the classroom that they will have to update their knowledge as the field of TESOL develops and also because they also realize that everything they need to be a successful language teacher cannot possibly be provided in their teacher education program. The field of TESOL has expanded a lot in the past 20 or so years and now there is also a growing recognition that the individual teacher is constantly shaping and reshaping his or her experiences and knowledge inside and outside the classroom. In the past, language teachers have been reliant either by their own will or outside force, on outside experts and what these experts tell them they should be doing in their classrooms even though they do not have knowledge of the context or the students. Language teachers have been expected to learn about their own teaching not by studying their unique experiences, but by looking at the findings of the outside experts. Teachers have been consumers of knowledge about practice rather than been producers of such knowledge. I am not saying that research by experts is not important and it has its place in helping teachers become better practitioners. Indeed as Van Lier (1994: 31) has noted, such research by experts in second language acquisition (SLA) theory or task-based language teaching (TBLT), or any other such ancillary to second language teaching and learning "is a valid an important pursuit." However we must also not forget that research on practical activities for practical purposes is equally important otherwise we may, as Van Lier reflected, find ourselves in a profession divided between those who "reflect without practicing, and those who practice without reflecting" (Van Lier, 1994: 31). To become a producer of such valid (in the sense that it is produced from that teacher's setting) reflections, language teachers will have to take on the role of reflective practitioner in their everyday professional practice.

(Re)Defining Reflective Practice

In the introduction and Chapter 1 of this book I noted that reflective practice can mean different things to different people and as a result there are many different definitions of reflective practice many of which I reproduced in Chapter 1 for you to consider. I did not define reflective practice in any of the preceding chapters on purpose because I had wanted readers to examine the material I have just presented in this book. I am now ready to define what reflective practice means to me and I hope readers will be able to see that my definition of reflective practice will be clearly understandable from the material I have presented in the previous chapters. Reflective practice is:

> A cognitive process accompanied by a set of attitudes in which teachers systematically collect data about their practice, and while engaging in dialogue with others use the data to make informed decisions about their practice both inside and outside the classroom.

REFERENCES

Acheson, K.A. and Gall, M.D. (1987) *Techniques in the clinical supervision of teachers*. New York: Longman.

Alger, C. (2008) Secondary teachers' conceptual metaphors of teaching and learning: Changes over the career span. *Teaching and Teacher Education* 25: 743–51.

Anzalone, F.M. (2010) Education for the law: reflective education for the law. In: Nona Lyons (ed.), *Handbook of reflective inquiry: Mapping a way of knowing for professional reflective inquiry*. New York: Springer, pp. 85–99.

Argyris, C. and Schön, D. (1974) *Theory in practice: increasing professional effectiveness*. Washington, DC: Jossey Bass.

Ashcraft, N. (2014) *Lesson planning*. Alexandria, Va, USA: TESOL International.

Association for Mindfulness in Education. (2008) Mindfulness in education: Laying the foundation for teaching and learning. www.mindfuleducation.org/ (accessed April 1, 2008).

Bailey, K.M. (2001) Action research, teacher research, and classroom research in language teaching. In: M. Celce-Murcia (ed.), *Teaching English as a second or foreign language* (3rd edn). Boston, MA: Heinle and Heinle, pp. 489–98.

Bailey, K.M. (2010) Observing classroom lessons for professional development. In: G. Park, H.P. Widodo, and A. Cirocki (eds), *Observation of teaching: Bridging theory and practice through research on teaching*. Munich, Germany: Lincom Europa, pp. 19–35.

Basturkmen. H. (2012) Review of research into the correspondence between language teachers' stated beliefs and practices. *System* 40(2): 282–95.

Barkhuizen, G., and Wette, R. (2008) Narrative frames for investigating the experiences of language teachers. *System* 36(3): 372–87.

Bartlett, L. (1990) Teacher development through reflective teaching. In: J.C. Richards and D. Nunan (eds), *Second language teacher education*. New York: Cambridge University Press, pp. 202–14.

Baurain, B. (2012) Beliefs into practice: a religious inquiry into teacher knowledge. *Journal of Language, Identity, and Education* 6: 201–19.

Block, D. (1992) Metaphors we teach and learn by. *Prospect* 7(3): 42–55.

Boud D., Keogh R. and Walker D. (1985) Promoting reflection in learning: A model. In: D. Boud, R. Keogh and D. Walker (eds), *Reflection: Turing Experience into Learning.* London: Kogan Page.

Brislin, R.W., Cushnew, K., Cherrie, C. and Young, M. (1986) *Intercultural interactions. A practical guide.* Thousand Oaks, CA: Sage.

Brookfield, S. (1990) *The skilful teacher.* San Francisco, CA: Jossey Bass.

Brookfield, S. (1995) *Becoming a critically reflective teacher.* San Francisco: Jossey-Bass.

Brookfield, S. (2006) *The skilful teacher* (2nd edn). San Francisco, CA: Jossey Bass.

Brown, R. (1998) The contemplative observer. *Educational Leadership* 56: 70–3.

Buchman, M. (1989) The careful vision: How practical is contemplation in teaching? *American Journal of Education* 78: 35–61.

Bullough, R.V. (1997) Practicing theory and theorizing practice in teacher education. In: J. Loughran and T. Russell (eds), *Teaching about teaching: Purpose, passion and pedagogy in teacher education.* London: Falmer Press, pp. 13–31.

Burns, A. (1995) Teacher-researchers: perspectives on teacher action research and curriculum renewal. In: A. Burns and S. Hood (eds), *Teachers' voices: exploring course design in a changing curriculum.* Sydney: NCELTR, Macquarie University, pp. 3–29.

Burns, A. (1999) *Collaborative action research for English language teachers.* Cambridge: Cambridge University Press.

Burns, A. and Richards, J. C. (eds) (2009) *The Cambridge guide to second language teacher education.* New York: Cambridge University Press.

Burton, J. (2009) Reflective practice. In: A. Burns and J.C. Richards (eds), *The Cambridge guide to second language teacher education.* Cambridge, UK: Cambridge University Press, pp. 298–307.

Calderhead, J. (1996) Teachers: Beliefs and knowledge. In: D. Berliner and R. Calfree (eds), *Handbook of educational psychology.* New York: Macmillan, pp. 709–25.

Cameron, L. and Low, G. (1999) Metaphor. *Language Teaching* 32: 77–96.

Carr, W. and Kemmis, S. (1985) *Becoming critical: Education, knowledge and action research.* Brighton: Falmer Press.

Carter, K. (1993) The place of story in the study of teaching and teacher education. *Educational Researcher* 22: 5–12.

Chaudron, C. (1988) *Second language classrooms: Research on teaching and learning.* Cambridge, UK: Cambridge University Press.

Chien, C. (2013) Analysis of a language teacher's journal of classroom practice as reflective practice. *Reflective Practice* 14(1): 131–43.

Cogan, M. (1973) *Clinical supervision.* Boston, MA: Houghton Mifflin.

Copeland, W.D., Birmingham, C., De La Cruz, E., and Lewin B. (1993) The reflective practitioner in teaching: toward a research agenda. *Teaching and Teacher Education* 9(4): 347–59.

Crookes, G. (1989) Grassroots action to improve ESL programs. *UH Working Papers in ESL,* 8(2): 45–61.

Crookes, G (2009) The practicality and relevance of second language critical pedagogy. *Language Teaching* 00: 1–16.

Crooks, G. (2013) *Critical ELT in action: foundations, promises, praxis.* New York: Routledge.

Crow, J. and Smith, L. (2005) Co-teaching in higher education: reflective conversations on shared experience as continued professional development for lecturers and health and social care students. *Reflective Practice* 6(4): 491–506.

Cruickshank, D, and Applegate, J. (1981). Reflective teaching as a strategy for teacher growth. *Educational Leadership* 38: 553–4.

Day, R. (1990) Teacher observation in second language teacher education. In: J.C. Richards and D. Nunan (eds), *Second language teacher education*. Cambridge: Cambridge University Press, pp.43–61.

Dewey, J. (1909) *Moral education*. Boston: Houghton Mifflin.

Dewey, J. (1933) *How we think: A restatement of the relation of reflective thinking to the educative process*. Boston: Houghton-Mifflin.

De Guerrero, M., and Villamil, O. (2000) Exploring ESL teachers' roles through metaphor analysis. *TESOL Quarterly* 34(2) 341–51.

DeMello, A. (1992) *Awareness*. New York: Doubleday.

Dickmeyer, N. (1989) Metaphor, model, and theory in education research. *Teachers College Record* 91: 151–60.

Edge, J. (ed.). (2001) *Action research*. Alexandria, Virginia: TESOL.

Edge, J. (2011) *The reflexive teacher educator in TESOL*. New York: Routledge.

Elbaz, F. (1991) Research on teachers' knowledge: the evolution of a discourse. *Journal of Curriculum Studies* 23: 1–19.

Elliot, J. (1991) *Action research for educational change*. Philadelphia: Open University Press.

Entwistle, N., Skinner, D., Entwistle, D., and Orr, S. (2000) Conceptions and beliefs about good teaching: an integration of contrasting research areas. *Higher Education Research & Development* 19(1): 5–26.

Farrell, T.S.C. (1999a) The reflective assignment: unlocking pre-service English teachers' beliefs on grammar teaching. *RELC Journal* 30: 1–17.

Farrell, T.S.C. (1999b) Reflective practice in an EFL teacher development group. *System* 27(2): 157–72.

Farrell, T.S.C. (2001) Tailoring reflection to individual needs. *Journal of Education for Teaching* 27(1): 23–38.

Farrell, T.S.C. (2004) *Reflective practice in action*. Thousand Oaks, CA: Corwin Press.

Farrell, T.S. C (2006) Reflective practice in action: a case study of a writing teacher's reflections on practice. *TESL Canada Journal* 23(2): 77–90.

Farrell, T.S.C. (2007a) *Reflective language teaching: From research to practice*. London: Continuum Press.

Farrell, T.S.C. (2007b) Failing the practicum: Narrowing the gap between expectation and reality with reflective practice. *TESOL Quarterly* 41(1): 193–201.

Farrell, T.S.C. (2010) Professional development through reflective practice IN and FOR action. In: G. Park, H.P. Widodo, and A. Cirocki (eds), *Observation of teaching: Bridging theory and practice through research on teaching*. Munich, Germany: Lincom Europa, pp. 37–47.

Farrell, T.S.C. (2011) 'Keeping SCORE': Reflective practice through classroom observations. *RELC Journal* 42(3): 265–72.

Farrell, T.S. C (2012) Reflecting on reflective practice: (Re) visiting Dewey and Schön. *TESOL Journal* 3(1): 7–16.

Farrell, T.S.C. (2013) *Reflective writing for language teachers*. London, UK: Equinox.

Farrell, T.S.C. (2014) *Reflective practice in ESL teacher development groups: from practices to principles*. Basingstoke, UK: Palgrave MacMillan.

Farrell, T.S. C (forthcoming) Reflecting on teacher-student relationships. *ELT Journal*

Farrell, T.S.C. and Ives, J. (forthcoming) Exploring teacher beliefs and classroom practices through reflective practice: a case study. *Language Teaching Research*

Farrell,T.S.C. and Bennis, K. (2013) Reflecting on ESL teacher beliefs and classroom practices: a case study. *RELC Journal* 44: 163–76.

Farrell,T.S.C. and Lim, P.C.P. (2005) Conceptions of grammar teaching: a case study of
teachers' beliefs and classroom practices. *TESL-EJ* 9(2): 1–13.

Fenstermacher, G.D. (1990) Some moral considerations on teaching as a profession. In: J.I.
Goodlad, R. Soder, and K.A. Sirotnik (eds), *The moral dimensions of teaching*. San Francisco: Jossey-Bass, pp. 130–51.

Fook, J. and Askeland, G. (2007) Challenges of critical reflection: 'nothing ventured, nothing gained.' *Social Work Education* 1: 1–14.

Francis, D. (1995) Reflective journal: a window to preservice teachers, practical knowledge.
Teaching and Teacher Education 11(3): 229–41.

Freeman, D. and Richards, J.C. (1993) Conceptions of teaching and the education of second language teachers. *TESOL Quarterly* 27: 193–216.

Gebhard, J.G. (1999). Reflecting through a teaching journal. In: J.G. Gebhard and R. Oprandy
(eds), *Language teaching awareness*, pp. 78–98.

Gebhard, J. and Oprandy, R. (1999) *Language teacher awareness*. New York: Cambridge University Press.

Ghaye, A. and Ghaye, K. (1998) *Teaching and learning through critical reflective practice*. London:
David Fulton Publishers.

Golombek, P.R. and Johnson, K.E. (2004) Narrative inquiry as a mediation space: examining emotional and cognitive dissonance in second-language teachers' development.
Teachers and Teaching: Theory and Practice 10(3): 307–27.

Good, T. and Brophy, J. (1991) *Looking into classrooms* (7th edn). New York: Longman.

Graves K (2008) The language curriculum: a social contextual perspective. *Language Teaching* 41(2): 147–81.

Hanh Thich Nhat (2006) The keys to the kingdom of God: New Year's Eve Dharma Talk.
www.mindfulnessbell.org/articles/keys.php (accessed December 12, 2013).

Hart, T.R. (2004) Opening the contemplative mind in the classroom. *Journal of Transformative Education* 2(1): 28–46.

Hatton, N. and Smith, D. (1995) Reflection in teacher education: towards definition and
implementation. *Teaching and Teacher Education* 11(1): 33–49.

Hooks, B. (1994) *Teaching to transgress: Education as the practice of freedom*. New York:
Routledge.

Hyde A.M. (2013) The yoga of critical discourse. *Journal of Transformative Education* 11(2):
114–26.

Jackson, J. (1997) Cases in TESOL teacher education: creating a forum for reflection. *TESL
Canada Journal* 14(2): 1–16.

Jackson, P. (1968) *Life in classrooms*. New York: Holt.

Jay, J.K. and Johnson, K.L. (2002) Capturing complexity: a typology of reflective practice
for teacher education. *Teaching and Teacher Education* 18: 73–85.

Johnston, B. (2003) *Values in English language teaching*. Mahwah, NJ: Lawrence Elbraum
Associates.

Johnson, K.E. (1991) The relationship between teachers' beliefs and practices during lit-
eracy instruction for non-native speakers of English. *Journal of Reading Behavior* 24(1):
83–108.

Johnson, K.E. (2009) *Second language teacher education: A sociocultural perspective*. New York:
Routledge.

Johnson, K.E. and Golombek, P. (2002) *Teacher's narrative inquiry as professional development.* New York: Cambridge University Press.

Johnson, K.E. and Golombek, P.R. (2011) The transformative power of narrative in second language teacher education. *TESOL Quarterly* 45(3): 486–509.

Josten, M.L. (2011) *Reflective thinking: A tool for professional development in educational practice.* (Doctoral Dissertation) Retrieved from UMI Dissertation Publishing. (UMI No. 3468504).

Kabat-Zinn, J., Lipworth, L. and Burney, R. (1985) The clinical use of mindfulness meditation for the self-regulation of chronic pain. *Journal of Behavioral Medicine* 8(2): 163–90.

Kelchtermans, G. (2009) Who I am in how I teach is the message. Self-understanding, vulnerability and reflection. *Teachers and Teaching: Theory and Practice* 15: 257–72.

Kember, D. (1997) A reconceptualisation of the research into university academics' conceptions of teaching. *Learning and Instruction* 7(3): 255–75.

Kemmis, S. and McTaggart, R. (1988) *The action research planner.* Geelong, Australia: Deakin University Press.

Kim, H., Clabo, L., Burbank, P. and Martins. M. (2010) Application of critical reflective inquiry in nursing education. In: Nona Lyons (ed.), *Handbook of reflective inquiry: Mapping a way of knowing for professional reflective inquiry.* New York: Springer, pp. 159–72.

Knezedivc, B. (2001) Action research. *IATEFL Teacher Development SIG Newsletter* 1: 10–12.

Kolb, D. (1984) *Experiential learning as the science of learning and development.* Englewood Cliffs, New York: Prentice Hall.

Kolb, D.A., and Fry, R. (1975) Towards an applied theory of experiential learning. In: C.L. Cooper (ed.), *Theories of group processes.* New York: Wiley, pp. 33–58.

Korthagen, F. (1985) Reflective teaching and preservice teacher education in the Netherlands. *Journal of Teacher Education* 9(3): 317–26.

Korthagen, F. (1993) Two modes of reflection. *Teaching and Teacher Education* 9: 317–26.

Kriesberg, S. (1992) *Transforming power: domination, empowerment, and education.* New York: SUNY Press.

Krishnamurti, J. (2009) *On knowing oneself.* Selected Texts.

Kumaravadivelu, B. (2012) *Language teacher education for a global. society: A modular model for knowing, analyzing, recognizing, doing, and seeing.* New York: Routledge.

Kuzborska, I. (2011) Links between teachers' beliefs and practices and research on reading. *Reading in a Foreign Language* 23(1): 102–28.

Lakeoff, G. and Johnson, M. (1980) *Metaphors we live by.* Chicago: University of Chicago Press.

Larrivee, B. (2008) Development of a tool to assess teachers' level of reflective practice. *Reflective Practice* 9(3): 341–60.

Lewin, K. (1943) Forces behind food habits and methods of change. *Bulletin of the National Research Council* 108: 35–65.

Lin, W., Shein, P. and Yang, S. (2012) Exploring personal EFL teaching metaphors in pre-service teacher education. *English Teaching: Practice and Critique* 11(1): 183–99.

Loughran, J. (2002) Effective reflective practice: in search of meaning in learning about teaching. *Journal of Teacher Education* 53(1): 33–43.

Lortie, D.C. (1975) *Schoolteacher: A sociological study.* Chicago: University of Chicago Press.

Luft, J. and Ingham, H. (1963) *Group processes: an introduction to group dynamics.* Palo Alto, CA: National Press Books.

Majid, F.A. (2008) Tracing decision-making from reflective journals: a case study of pre-service teachers. In: M. Kabilan and M. Vethamani (eds), *Qualitative studies on English language development.* Kuala Lumpur: Sasbadi, pp. 8–44.

McCabe, A. (2002) Narratives: a wellspring for development. In: J. Edge (ed.) *Continuing professional development*. UK: IATEFL, pp. 82–9.

McGregor, D. (1960) *The human side of enterprise*. New York: McGraw-Hill.

Meddings L. and Thornbury S. (2009) *Teaching unplugged: Dogme in English language teaching*. Peaslake, UK: Delta Publishing.

Merton, T. (1959) *The secular journal of Thomas Merton*. New York, Farrar, Straus & Cudahy.

Miller, J.P. (1994) *The contemplative practitioner: Meditation in education and the professions*. Toronto: OISE Press.

Nishino, T. (2012) Modeling teacher beliefs and practices in context: a multimethods approach. *The Modern Language Journal* 96(3): 380–99.

Oberg, A, and Blades, C. (1990) The spoken and the unspoken: the story of an educator. *Phenomonology+Pedagogy* 8: 161–80.

Olshtain, E. and Kupferberg, I. (1998) Relective-narrative discourse of FL teachers exhibits professional knowledge. *Language Teaching Research* 2: 185–202.

Oprandy, R. Golden, L. and Shiomi, K. (1999) Teachers talking about teaching. In: J. Gebhard and R. Oprandy (eds), *Language teaching awareness*. New York: Cambridge University Press, pp. 149–71.

Oxford, R.L., Tomlinson, S., Barcelos, A., Harrington, C., Lavine, R. Z., Saleh, A. and Longhini, A. (1998) Clashing metaphors about classroom teachers: toward a systematic typology for the language teaching field. *System* 26(1): 3–50.

Pajak, E.F. (1986) Psychoanalysis, teaching, and supervision. *Journal of Curriculum and Supervision* 1: 122–31.

Palmer, P.J. (1998) *The courage to teach*. San Francisco: Jossey-Bass.

Pajares, M.F. (1992) Teachers' beliefs and educational research: cleaning up a messy construct. *Review of Educational Research* 62: 307–32.

Perfecto, M.R. (2008) Teachers' beliefs system and their professional development training: the case of four teachers in Philippine secondary schools. In: M. Kabilan and M. Vethamani (eds), *Qualitative studies on English language development*. Kuala Lumpur: Sasbadi, pp. 45–74.

Phipps, S. and Borg, S. (2009) Exploring tensions between teachers' grammar teaching beliefs and practices. *System* 37(3): 380–90.

Polanyi, M. (1962) *Personal knowledge: Towards a post-critical philosophy*. Chicago: University of Chicago Press.

Polanyi, M. (1967) *The tacit dimension*. Chicago: University of Chicago Press.

Pratt, D.D. (1992) Conceptions of teaching. *Adult Education Quarterly* 42(4): 203–20.

Richards, J. (1990) Beyond training: approaches to teacher education in language teaching. *Language Teacher* 14: 3–8.

Richards, J.C. (1996) Teachers' maxims in language teaching. *TESOL Quarterly* 30: 281–96.

Richards, J.C. (1998) *Beyond training*. New York: Cambridge University Press.

Richards, J.C. (2013) Curriculum approaches in language teaching: forward, central, and backward design. *RELC Journal* 44(1): 5–33.

Richards, J.C. and Lockhart, C. (1994) *Reflective teaching*. New York: Cambridge University Press.

Richards. J.C. and Farrell, T.S.C. (2005) *Professional development for language teachers*. New York: Cambridge University Press.

Richards, J.C., Gallo, P.B., Renandya, W.A. (2001) Exploring teachers' beliefs and the processes of change. *PAC Journal* 1: 41–58.

Richardson, L. (1997) *Fields of play: Constructing an academic life.* New Brunswick, NJ: Rutgers University Press.

Robbins, P. (1991) *How to plan and implement a peer coaching programme.* Alexandra, VA: ASCD.

Rolfe, G., Freshwater, D. and Jasper M. (2011) *Critical reflection in practice* (2nd edn). Basingstoke: Palgrave.

Roeser, R.W. and Peck, S.C. (2009) An education in awareness: self, motivation, and self-regulated learning in contemplative perspective. *Educational Psychologist* 44: 119–36.

Rogers, C.R. (1967) *A therapist's view of psychotherapy.* London: Constable.

Sarbin, T. (1986) The narrative as a root metaphor for psychology. In: T.R. Sarbin (ed.), *Narrative psychology: The storied nature of human conduct.* New York: Praeger, pp. 3–21.

Schön, D.A. (1983) *The reflective practitioner: How professionals think in action.* New York: Basic Books.

Schön, D.A. (1987) *Educating the reflective practitioner: Towards a new design for teaching and learning in the profession.* San Francisco: Jossey-Bass.

Scholes, R. (1981) Language, narrative, and anti-narrative. In: W.J.T. Mitchell (ed.), *On narrative.* Chicago: University of Chicago Press, pp. 200–8.

Senge, P., Scharmer, C.O., Jaworski, J. and Flowers, B.S. (2004) *Presence: an exploration of profound change in people, organizations, and society.* New York: Doubleday

Senior, R. (2006) *The experience of language teaching.* New York: Cambridge University Press.

Seidel, J. (2006) Some thoughts on teaching as contemplative practice. *Teachers College Record* 108: 1901–14.

Shapiro, S.B. and Reiff, J. (1993) A framework for reflective inquiry on practice: beyond intuition and experience. *Psychological Reports* 73: 1379–94.

Shulman, J. (ed.) (1992) *Case methods in teacher education.* New York: Teachers College Press.

Smith, E. (2011) Teaching critical reflection. *Teaching in Higher Education* 16(2): 211–23.

Stanley, C. (1998) A framework for teacher reflectivity. *TESOL Quarterly* 32(3): 584–91.

Stem, H.H. (1983) *Fundamental concepts of language teaching.* Oxford: Oxford University Press.

Struman, P. (1992) Team teaching: a case study from Japan. In: D. Nunan (ed.), *Collaborative language learning and teaching.* Cambridge: Cambridge University Press, pp. 141–61.

Taba, H. (1962) *Curriculum development: Theory and practice.* New York: Harcourt Brace and World.

Tabachnik, R. and Zeichner, K. (2002) Reflections on reflective teaching. In: A. Pollard (ed.), *Readings for reflective teaching.* London: Continuum, pp. 13–16.

Taggart, G. and Wilson, A.P. (1998) *Promoting reflective thinking in teachers.* Thousand Oaks, CA: Corwin Press.

Thepyanmongkol, P. (2012) *A study guide for the right practice of the Three Trainings* (3rd edn). Bangkok, Thailand: The National Coordination Institute of Meditation Institutes of Thailand.

Thiel, T. (1999) Reflections on critical incidents. *Prospect* 14: 44–52.

Thompson, A.G. (1992) Teachers' beliefs and conceptions: a synthesis of the research. In: D.A. Grouws (ed.), *Handbook of research on mathematics teaching and learning.* New York: Macmillan, pp. 127–46.

Tom, A.R. (1980) Teaching as a moral craft: a metaphor for teaching and teacher education. *Curriculum Inquiry* 10(3): 317–23.

Tom, A.R. (1984) *Teaching as a moral craft.* New York: Longman.

Tom, A.R. (1986) *Bloomsbury's prophet: G.E. Moore and the development of his moral philosophy.* Philadephia: Temple University Press.

Tsui, A. (1995) Exploring collaborative supervision in in-service teacher education. *Journal of Curriculum and Supervision* 10(4): 346–71.

Ur, P. (1992) Teacher learning. *ELT Journal* 46(1): 56–61.

Valli, L. (1997) Listening to other voices: a description of teacher reflection in the United States. *Peabody Journal of Education* 72(1): 67–88.

Van Lier, L. (1994) Action research. *Sintagma* 6: 31–7.

Van Manen, M. (1977) Linking ways of knowing with ways of being practical. *Curriculum Inquiry* 6: 205–28.

Van Manen, M. (1991) *The tact of teaching: The meaning of pedagogical thoughtfulness.* Albany, NY: SUNY Press.

Vaughan, F. (ed.) (1979) *Beyond ego: The transpersonal dimensions in psychology.* Los Angeles: J.P. Tarcher.

Wajnryb, R. (1992) *Classroom observation tasks.* Cambridge: Cambridge University Press.

Wallace, M.J. (1991) *Teacher training: A reflective approach.* Cambridge: Cambridge University Press.

Wallace, M. (1998) *Action research for language teachers.* Cambridge: Cambridge University Press.

Wassermann, S. (1993) *Getting down to cases: Learning to teach with case studies.* New York: Teachers College.

Widdowson, H.G. (1984) The incentive value of theory in teacher education. *ELT Journal* 38(2): 86–90.

Wiggins, G. and McTighe, J. (2005) *Understanding by design* (2nd edn). Alexandria, Virginia: Association for Supervision and Curriculum Development.

Wilkins, E. (2009) Revisiting the list of Richard's maxims. http://ows.edb.utexas.edu/site/teaching-russian-e-portfolio/revisiting-list-richards-maxims (accessed January 13, 2014).

Woods, D. (1996) *Teacher cognition in language teaching.* Cambridge: Cambridge University Press.

Yang, S. (2009) Using blogs to enhance critical reflection and community of practice. *Educational Technology & Society* 12(2): 11–21.

Zahorik, J. (1986) Acquiring teaching skills. *Journal of Teacher Education* 27(2): 21–5.

Zeichner, K.M. and Liston, D.P. (1996) *Reflective teaching: an introduction.* Mahwah, New Jersey: Lawrence Erlbaum Associates.

Zwozdiak-Myers, P. (2012) *The teacher's reflective practice handbook. Becoming an extended professional through capturing evidence-informed practice.* London and New York: Routledge.

INDEX

Note: 'f' after a page number indicates a figure; 't' indicates a table.